From Vine to Table

The Unexpected Joy of Zucchini's Magic

by
CHRISTINA *Cavallaro* **EDICK**

Copyright © 2019 by Christina Cavallaro Edick

Cover and interior design by Masha Shubin
Photos © Christina Cavallaro Edick
Bigstock.com: Watercolor Zucchini © characters for your; Zucchini Sketches © Iamnee; Delicate Pattern © Kannaa. Design Cuts: Handdrawn Fancy Shape © Julia Dreams.

All rights reserved. No part of this book may be reproduced or transmitted in any form or by any means whatsoever, including photocopying, recording or by any information storage and retrieval system, without written permission from the publisher and/or author. Contact Cucinare Libri at CucinareLibri.com.

Publisher: Cucinare Libri | www.CucinareLibri.com

Paperback ISBN-13 978-1-7336968-1-4 | ISBN-10 1-7336968-1-4
eBook ISBN-13 978-1-7336968-0-7 | ISBN-10 1-7336968-0-6

5 7 9 11 12 10 8 6 4

Dedication

The zucchini in our summer garden grew and multiplied many times over, resulting in an abundant crop. While we love zucchini, our plants produced much more than we could possibly eat.

So the big giveaway began. Book club, writing class, weekly game day crowd, library meetings, swim buddies, any and all were invited — make that strongly encouraged — to take one or more zucchini home. If neighbors were walking their dog or picking up mail at the receptacle in front of our house, I ran out and offered zucchini. I left them on neighbors' doorsteps. I even raffled off several at an Italian club meeting. First prize was "my baby" weighing in at 8 pounds 7 ounces.

It did get a little ridiculous as neighbors and friends began avoiding me when I showed up with zucchini in hand. So my only chance to salvage this plentiful harvest was to slice, dice, and cook them.

This book is dedicated to all the summer gardeners who planted too many zucchini AND the recipients of zucchini from friends and family with abundant gardens.

Table of Contents

Introduction 1

Breakfast
Three Cheese Vegetable Frittata 5
Zucchini Banana Flaxseed Muffins 7
Zucchini Waffles 9
Ricotta Zucchini Pancakes 11
Baked Egg Zucchini Nests 13
Egg Sandwich 15
Apple Oat Breakfast Muffin 17

Appetizers & Snacks
Turkey Ricotta Meatballs 21
Zucchini Hummus Dip 23
Great Balls of Zucchini 25
Panelle 27
Think Outside the Box Zucchini Nachos 29
    Crisp Zucchini Chips 31
Baba Ganoush 33
Fruit Leather 35

Soups & Sauce
Zoup 39
Vegetable Soup With Pizzazz 41
Minestrone 42
Zucchini Corn Chowder 45
Chili 47
Ciambotta or Giambotta 49
Zucchini Pasta Sauce 51

Salads
Garden Vegetable Potato Salad 55
Mediterranean Pasta Salad 57
Vegetable Slaw Salad 59
Quinoa Vegetable Salad 61
Grilled Corn, Cucumber & Tomato Salad 63
Zucchini and Veggie Stir-Fry Salad 65

Main Dishes
Houdini Zucchini Disguised as Lasagna 69
Mediterranean Pizza 71
Sicilian Caponata Marries Pasta 73
Chicken Stir-Fry 75
Greek Turkey Burgers 77
Chicken Artichoke With Zucchini Ribbons 78
Beef Enchiladas & Burrito Boats 80
    Beef Enchiladas 81
    Burrito Boats 83
Bacon, Zucchini, & Tomato Sandwich 85
Farro Casserole 87

Side Dishes
Zucchini Corn Fritters 91
Squash Blossoms Stuffed With Ricotta 92
Sicilian Caponata 95
Tater Zots 97
No Hassle Hasselback Zucchini 99
Fifty Shades of Color in Garden Vegetables 101
Vegetable Galette 102
Zucchini Gratinato 105
Easy Cheesy Zucchini Rice 107

Breads, Muffins & More

- Old-Fashioned Zucchini Bread 111
- Carrot Apple Zucchini Bread 113
- Zucchini Lemon Bread 115
- Blueberry Yogurt Zucchini Bread 117
- Snickerdoodle Swirl Bread 119
- Cinnamon Roll Zucchini Bread 120
- Chocolate Zucchini Muffins 123
- Cheesy Zucchini Biscuits 125
- Cornbread Muffins 127
- Light and Savory Courgette Scones 129

Desserts

- Oat Nut Chocolate Chip Cookies 132
  - Limoncello Glaze 133
- Chocolate Zookies 135
- Lemon Ricotta Cookies 137
- Traditional Ziggy Figgy Bars 139
- Gluten-Free Ziggy Figgy Bars 141
- Brownies 143
- Limoncello Cake 145
- Cheesecake Cupcakes 147
- Walnut Shortbread Bites 149

Condiments

- Zesto (Zucchini Pesto) 153
- Sweet Relish 155
- Strawberry Pineapple Jelly 157
- Pico de Gallo 159
- Zucchini Spread 161

Tips

- Conversion Charts 167

About the Author 171

Acknowledgments

Heartfelt thanks go out to all who helped with this book.

Cheri Papini, gardener extraordinaire, whose green thumb and greenhouse started my zucchini plants with love from seeds. Thank you for sharing your healthy plants!

- To those who took some zucchini when the harvest overwhelmed me, I am especially grateful.
- The many taste testers of recipes get a special thank-you for giving feedback and suggestions.
- A shout out to my friends who put up with me during this book writing/recipe creation process, ignoring the fact that even my hair was turning green (which we all swear was due to eating zucchini at every meal for four months, not the fact that I swim every day in the summer).
- Patricia B-J and Carol W cleaned up more than a few sentences in the book with their sharp editing skills and English grammar background.
- A special acknowledgment goes to Ellis B for sharing his knowledge and experience publishing books.

And I couldn't have written this book without the encouragement of my husband, who was extremely patient and understanding when I put another variation of zucchini in front of him, trying out yet another zucchini recipe. He cleaned up the kitchen after my experiments, most of the time my having used every pot, pan, and measuring utensil we own. He never complained, and was especially happy when I made his zucchini favorites — bread, cookies, and brownies.

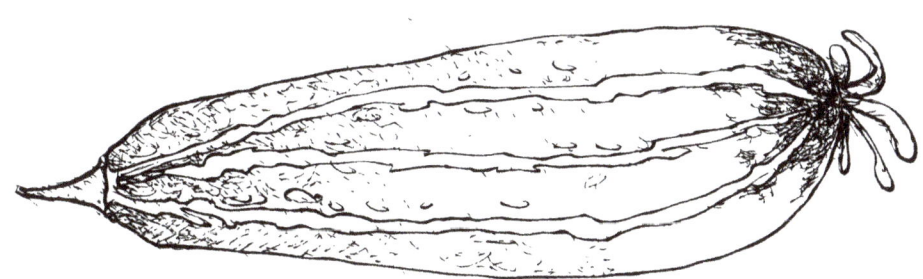

Introduction

I confess I'm a person who "lives to eat" more than "eats to live."

I have a passion for food. Cooking and experiencing food as a love of life was ingrained in me as a child growing up in an Italian-American family. We have always had a backyard garden and use the fresh fruits, vegetables, and herbs in our meals.

I equate most of my everyday experiences to food. In case you don't think that way, here are some examples: Our house backs up to a golf course and if a golf ball lands in our yard, I might think about making meatballs. Or if I watch a movie with an Italian theme, I want to make homemade pasta or some other Italian dish to re-experience the feelings I had when watching the movie.

Nicole Gulotta, author of *Eat This Poem*, a cookbook pairing poetry and food, is a writer with a similar inclination to mine, relating life experiences to meals shared around a table. She writes:

> Food memories are inescapable. They are chosen for us, given flavor and meaning before we are old enough to learn the names of the ingredients.

Janet Theophano, author of *Eat My Words: Reading Women's Lives Through the Cookbooks They Wrote*, explains:

> As cooks, we must first taste a dish in our imaginations, see it on the table, share it with guests—sometimes more fanciful than real—and then actually reproduce it from a text. A longing for the pleasures of the table reflects a concern for balance and harmony and an integration of the physical and spiritual nature of our existence. In this way, cookbooks are a meditation. Preparing a dish or a meal is not merely an effort to satisfy physical hunger but often a quest for the good life.

***

Well Christina (that fine cooking genie)
Is now known as the Queen of Zucchini~!
With courgettes she'll find
Ways to just blow your mind
Like that other great wizard, Houdini

By Paul Raworth Bennett

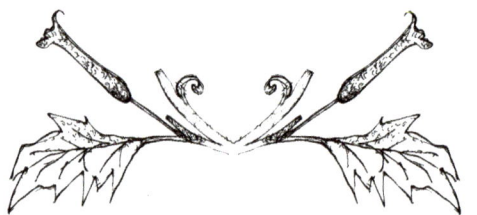

Three Cheese Vegetable Frittata

Frittatas can be baked or fried. If I'm just making an individual serving or two, I throw all the ingredients into a small frypan and I cover it with a lid about midway through cooking. If making a larger frittata serving 4+ people, baking it in a 350°F oven for 35 minutes or so is a good option. Either method results in a flavorful and robust egg dish to serve any time of day.

This recipe was created so I could use cooked zucchini, asparagus, and leftover challah bread. It's also a good recipe if you need to use up leftover pasta!

Serves 2.

INGREDIENTS

- 2 pieces of bacon, pancetta, or 1 Italian sausage diced or chopped
- ¼ cup onion, chopped
- ½ cup bread cubes or cooked pasta (leave out these ingredients for gluten free)
- 1 cup egg white substitute (or 4 whole eggs if you prefer)
- ⅓ cup shredded mozzarella cheese
- ¼ cup grated Parmesan
- ¼ cup ricotta cheese, store brand or homemade (see Tips for homemade ricotta cheese recipe resource) or substitute cottage cheese
- ½ cup cooked vegetables (any combination of zucchini, eggplant, asparagus, broccoli, or spinach)
- ¼ cup milk, if needed
- Olive oil for frying
- Salt and pepper to taste

INSTRUCTIONS FOR FRYPAN METHOD

1. Sauté bacon or sausage and onions until bacon is crisp and onions are translucent. Set aside. Drain most of the grease, leaving a little to cook with.
2. Add pasta or bread to the frypan and sauté for a minute or two (if using).
3. Mix eggs with cheeses and cooked vegetables. Add milk if mixture needs more moisture.
4. Put all ingredients back in the frypan to cook together.
5. After a few minutes, add a lid to help set the eggs.
6. Frittata is done when eggs are set, not runny or gooey.

BREAKFAST

Zucchini Banana Flaxseed Muffins

Who says healthy recipes can't be tasty and easy to make? And don't let the flaxseed in this recipe scare you away. My "I don't eat muffins, especially healthy ones" hubby ate several of these. Did I tell him they were good for him and contained zucchini? Of course not! I served them to him in a dimly lit room so he couldn't see what was in the muffin itself.

Makes 24 mini muffins or 15 regular sized muffins, or 12 regular sized muffins plus 1 mini loaf.

INGREDIENTS

- ½ cup regular rolled oats
- 2 tablespoons packed brown sugar
- 2 tablespoons butter, melted
- 1¼ cups whole wheat flour
- ½ cup oat flour (or substitute all-purpose flour)
- ⅓ cup granulated sugar
- ¼ cup flaxseed meal (I used Bob's Red Mill®; see Flaxseed in Tips for more information about flaxseed)
- 1½ teaspoons baking powder
- 1 teaspoon ground cinnamon
- ½ teaspoon salt
- ½ teaspoon baking soda
- 2 eggs, lightly beaten
- ¾ cup fat-free milk (ok to substitute whole milk)
- 2 tablespoons canola oil (ok to substitute applesauce)
- ½ cup finely shredded unpeeled zucchini (moisture squeezed out)
- ⅓ cup mashed banana (about 1 small-medium banana)

INSTRUCTIONS

Prep: Preheat oven to 400°F. Lightly coat 24 mini muffin cups or 15 2½" muffin cups, or 12 2½" muffin cups and 1 mini loaf pan with cooking spray.

1. In a small bowl stir together oats, brown sugar, and melted butter. Set aside for topping.
2. In a medium bowl stir together next 8 ingredients (up to and including baking soda).
3. In another small bowl combine remaining 5 ingredients. Add egg mixture all at once to the dry ingredients. Stir just until moistened (batter should be slightly lumpy).
4. Spoon batter into prepared muffin cups, filling each about two-thirds full. Sprinkle oat mixture over the batter. If making 12 2½" muffins there will be batter left over, enough for 1 mini loaf or a few more muffins. Pour leftover batter into mini loaf pan or a few more muffin cups, whichever is your preference.
5. Bake from 12 to 15 minutes for mini muffins, 20 minutes or until golden for regular sized muffins, and about 30 minutes if using the mini loaf pan.
6. Cool in muffin cups (and mini loaf pan) on a wire rack for 5 minutes. Remove from muffin cups (and mini loaf pan). Serve warm.

Zucchini Waffles

For the non–green vegetable lovers, I tried waffling zucchini. I read an article about a mother who was trying to get her children to eat dinner. They were picky eaters but loved waffles, so she waffled the dinner ingredients and they ate it! After you have tasted this recipe, you may agree this is a great way to eat zucchini.

These "waffles" could be cut in pieces and used as appetizers, served with eggs for breakfast, or work as a side dish for dinner. The possibilities are almost endless.

Serves 4.

INGREDIENTS

2 cups shredded zucchini (roughly 2 medium zucchini)	Nonstick cooking spray
1 large egg	¼ teaspoon salt
¼ cup milk	¼ teaspoon pepper
½ cup grated parmesan	Light sprinkle of garlic powder
½ cup all-purpose flour	Light sprinkle of onion powder

INSTRUCTIONS

Prep: Preheat the waffle iron to medium and the oven or warming tray to its lowest setting.

1. Squeeze zucchini dry in a clean tea towel.
2. Whisk together the egg, milk, and the grated parmesan in a large bowl.
3. Combine the flour with about ¼ teaspoon salt and ¼ teaspoon freshly ground black pepper, and a light sprinkle of garlic powder and onion powder.
4. Mix together the egg and milk mixture with the dry ingredients (flour and cheese).
5. Add zucchini and fold in until everything is well combined.
6. Coat the waffle iron with nonstick spray.
7. Measure out rounded tablespoons of batter (or more depending on the size of your waffle iron).
8. Put batter in the waffle iron, leaving room for it to spread slightly.
9. Close the lid and cook until browned, about 3–4 minutes, or according to your waffle iron instructions.

Ricotta Zucchini Pancakes

Ricotta Zucchini Pancakes are not only tasty – you also get a shot of protein and fiber in every bite. If you are not a ricotta fan, you can substitute plain Greek yogurt.

Flaxseeds are a great source of dietary fiber and are a plant-based protein. There are many benefits to including flaxseed in recipes. (See Flaxseed in Tips for more information.)

INGREDIENTS

- 1 cup all-purpose flour
- 1 tablespoon flaxseed meal (I used Bob's Red Mill®)
- ½ teaspoon baking soda
- ¼ teaspoon salt
- 1–2 tablespoons granulated sugar (depending on how sweet you like it – I used 1½ tablespoons)
- 1 tablespoon brown sugar
- 1½ teaspoons cinnamon
- ⅛ teaspoon nutmeg
- Dash of allspice
- 2 eggs
- ½ cup ricotta or plain Greek yogurt (nonfat, low-fat or full fat)
- 1½ cups zucchini, chopped fine (optional: remove skin)
- ½ teaspoon vanilla
- 1 tablespoon olive oil
- ⅓–½ cup milk (to thin batter)

INSTRUCTIONS

Prep: Preheat griddle to 375–400°F.

1. Mix dry ingredients together and set aside.
2. Combine wet ingredients and slowly add to dry ingredients, carefully incorporating everything together.
3. Butter griddle lightly. Pour pancake batter onto the griddle to create the size pancake you like. I use ¼ cup.
4. Cook on one side for a minute or two, until the bottom browns. Flip and finish cooking on the opposite side.

Serve with maple syrup or your favorite jam. (See Condiments for Strawberry Pineapple Jelly recipe.)

Baked Egg Zucchini Nests

Baked Egg Nests are a great way to eat zucchini for breakfast. The egg sits inside the nest and if there are extra empty nests, they can be used as a side dish to the main egg nest, or served at dinner stuffed with rice, pasta, or mashed potatoes. Kids love them stuffed with scrambled eggs and cheese.

Serves 6.

INGREDIENTS

- 2 cups zucchini, shredded
- 1–2 teaspoons onion, grated
- ½ teaspoon salt
- ¼ teaspoon pepper
- 2 tablespoons egg white (about 1 egg separated)
- ½ ounce cheddar cheese, grated
- 6 eggs
- Options: Top with bacon, extra cheese and pico de gallo. Also can add dollop of fresh ricotta (see Condiment for pico de gallo and Tips for homemade ricotta recipe resource).

INSTRUCTIONS

Prep: Preheat oven to 400°F. Spray 6-cup muffin pan with cooking oil. Squeeze zucchini in tea towel to remove moisture.

1. Combine zucchini, onion, salt, pepper, egg white and cheese.
2. Press zucchini mixture into the muffin tin, pushing into the bottom and up the sides with your fingers or tamp down using the bottom of a small glass.
3. Bake 15–20 minutes or until golden brown. Remove from the oven.
4. Crack an egg into each muffin cup.
5. Bake 12–15 minutes to achieve a cooked yolk. Bake less for softer yolk.

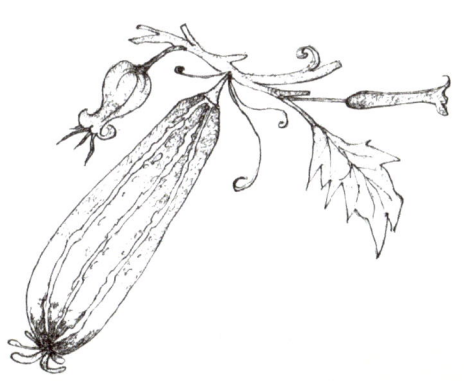

BREAKFAST

Egg Sandwich

Fast food breakfast sandwich? Not on my watch! This egg sandwich is heads above any fast food version in flavor, and nutrition. And you don't have to limit eating this sandwich to breakfast time only. It's good any time of day.

Makes 2 sandwiches.

INGREDIENTS

- 4 pieces of bread, toasted (I used Dave's Killer Bread)
- 2–3 tablespoons zucchini spread (see Condiments for recipe)
- 2 whole eggs
- 2 slices of bacon (turkey, applewood, pepper, or your favorite)
- 1 tomato, sliced
- 2 slices red onion
- 2 tablespoons mozzarella, shredded or sliced
- Optional: drizzle of pepper sauce

INSTRUCTIONS

1. Toast bread, and butter with zucchini spread or substitute a slice of zucchini sautéed in olive oil until softened for the spread.
2. Fry bacon to crispish. Add red onion to frypan to wilt.
3. Fry or poach egg to your preferred doneness.
4. Assemble sandwich by layering zucchini (if using instead of spread), bacon, tomato, and onion on the bread. Top with egg.
5. Sprinkle cheese on top of egg and drizzle pepper sauce if using.

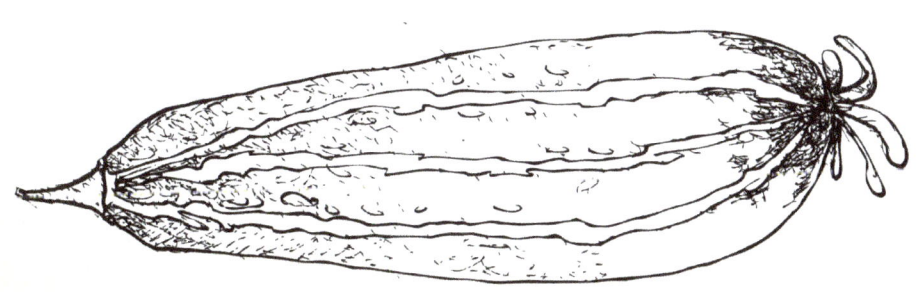

BREAKFAST

Apple Oat Breakfast Muffin

Grab-and-go apple oat breakfast muffins – perfect in the morning! It's tough to fix and eat a full breakfast some mornings before running out to the gym, getting the kids off to school, or entering the slug of freeway traffic to get to work on time. With these muffins on hand, you could grab one and get on with your morning activities. Kids love them and they freeze well too!

Makes 12 regular sized muffins.

INGREDIENTS

- 1 cup oatmeal
- 1½ cups all-purpose flour
- 2 teaspoons baking powder
- 1 teaspoon salt
- ⅓ to ½ cup sugar (depends on how sweet you like your muffins)
- 2 heaping teaspoons cinnamon
- 1 cup milk
- 2 eggs
- 2 apples, peeled, cored and finely chopped
- 1 cup zucchini, shredded and squeezed dry to measure ½ cup
- 2 tablespoons canola oil (option: substitute coconut oil)

INSTRUCTIONS

Prep: Preheat oven to 375°F. Spray 12-cup muffin tin with cooking oil.

1. Blend dry ingredients together: flour, oatmeal, sugar, baking powder, salt and cinnamon
2. Whisk wet ingredients: eggs, milk, oil, apples and zucchini.
3. Fold wet ingredients into dry ingredients.
4. Pour into muffin tin and bake for 30–35 minutes or until firm. Cool on wire rack for 10 minutes.

Turkey Ricotta Meatballs

These meatballs are perfect for snacking as well as adding to a meal with pasta sauce. Another way to enjoy these meatballs is to make them miniature sized (about ½" diameter) to use in soup or on pizza.

Meatball yield depends on meatball size.

INGREDIENTS

- 1 cup zucchini, shredded
- 1 pound ground turkey
- 2 tablespoons ricotta, store brand or homemade (see Tips for recipe resource)
- 1 egg
- ½ cup bread crumbs
- ½ cup parmesan cheese, grated
- 2 cloves garlic, minced
- 1 tablespoon fresh parsley, chopped fine
- 1 tablespoon fresh basil, chopped fine
- ¼ teaspoon crushed red pepper
- ⅛ teaspoon salt

INSTRUCTIONS

Prep: Preheat oven to 350°F and line a baking sheet with non-stick foil or parchment paper.

1. Squeeze zucchini in cheesecloth or tea towel until zucchini is dry.
2. Combine all ingredients in a bowl and mix well.
3. Shape mixture into round meatball shapes and place on a baking sheet.
4. Bake 30 minutes for average 1½–2" meatballs. (Bake less time for mini meatballs.) Meatballs are done when meat thermometer reaches 165°F.
5. Meatballs may look undercooked but if they measure 165°F, they will be done.

Zucchini Hummus Dip

Hummus is the perfect party appetizer. Did you know that the word "hummus" comes from the Arabic word meaning "chickpeas"? There are no chickpeas in this recipe but we can keep that our little secret and still refer to it as hummus. And if you feel you need to, you can substitute chickpeas for the cannellini beans.

Serve with chips, crackers and dipping vegetables.

INGREDIENTS

- 1 pound of zucchini, quartered lengthwise
- 2 tablespoons olive oil
- 2 tablespoons sesame seeds, toasted
- 1 teaspoon lemon zest
- 1½ teaspoons lemon juice (about 1 lemon)
- 1 clove garlic
- Dash of garlic herb seasoning
- 1 can cannellini beans, drained and rinsed
- ¼ cup pine nuts, toasted
- Drizzle of olive oil
- Salt and pepper

INSTRUCTIONS

1. In a large bowl toss the zucchini with oil and season with salt and pepper.
2. Heat a grill to medium and grill the zucchini until tender and charred in spots, turning often to prevent burning (5–10 minutes). Refrigerate to cool.
3. In a food processor puree the zucchini and the rest of the ingredients, except olive oil.
4. Drizzle olive oil into food processor as it is pureeing zucchini mixture into the consistency of hummus.
5. Transfer to a bowl. Top with additional pine nuts and an additional drizzle of olive oil if desired.

APPETIZERS & SNACKS

Great Balls of Zucchini

Jerry Lee Lewis' signature song "Great Balls of Fire" was playing in the background. What a song to get you pumped up and motivated. Since I was going to be cooking zucchini again, I needed some motivation! And that song gave me the idea to make zucchini balls. I warned you I experience life through food.

These zucchini balls make great appetizers, can be added into pasta sauce, plated as a side dish smothered in mozzarella, or served with spaghetti, or, or, or…

The number of servings depends on the size you make the balls. Recipe can easily be cut in half.

INGREDIENTS

½ red onion, chopped

½ white onion, chopped

2–3 garlic cloves, minced

8 cups zucchini, chopped

2 tablespoons parsley, chopped

1 tablespoon basil, chopped

2 eggs

½ cup pecorino cheese, shredded

1 cup mozzarella, shredded

¾ to 1 cup breadcrumbs

Few dashes of hot sauce (optional)

Few dashes of garlic herb blend

Salt and pepper to taste

Olive oil and canola oil

INSTRUCTIONS

1. Sauté onions and garlic in a small amount of olive oil for about 2 to 3 minutes and then add the zucchini. Cook together over a medium/high heat for about 5 minutes or until zucchini softens. Add a few dashes of salt and black pepper to taste. (Add pepper sauce at this point if you want a little zing.)

2. Remove zucchini mixture from the pan and scoop it into a strainer that is over a bowl. This is necessary to let some of the moisture drain out. Allow zucchini to drain and cool for about 15 minutes.

3. Add the zucchini mixture to a bowl along with 2 eggs, pecorino cheese, mozzarella cheese, breadcrumbs, parsley and basil, and mix all together. Form into balls.

4. Add some breadcrumbs to a dish and roll the balls in them to coat thoroughly.

5. Fill a deep skillet with enough oil to cover the zucchini balls using a combination of one-half canola oil and one-half olive oil. Heat the oil over a medium flame.

6. Gently add the zucchini balls into the hot oil and fry for a few minutes on each side, until browned. Be sure to turn the balls while frying to cook evenly.

7. Remove balls from the skillet and place on a paper towel–lined dish to soak up the excess oil.

Best served warm but also good served at room temperature.

Panelle

(Sicilian Street Food With Chickpea & Veggies)

The popular street food (found in Palermo, Sicily) called panelle is a favorite of mine. (Sicily is where half of my Italian roots can be found.) I've not found a restaurant in California or Oregon that serves panelle. If you are unfamiliar with this delightful fritter, here is what Wikipedia has to say about them:

> Panelle (or panella di ceci) are Sicilian fritters made from chickpea flour and other ingredients. Panelle are believed to be of Arab origin. They are a popular street food in Palermo and are often eaten between slices of bread or on a roll, like a sandwich.
>
> Sicilian cuisine shows traces of all cultures that have existed on the island over the last two millennia. Although its cuisine has a lot in common with Italian cuisine, Sicilian food also has Greek, Spanish, French, and Arab influences.

Ingredients for panelle are usually just a combination of chickpea flour and water. My version was created to add some depth of flavor and as a way to use garden vegetables (particularly zucchini). The vegetables do add a bit more moisture to the batter, so pat dry before mixing with the chickpea flour and frying.

INGREDIENTS

- 2 cups chickpea flour (can be purchased at Walmart or Bob's Red Mill®)
- 2½–3 cups water
- ½ small red onion, grated
- 1 medium-large carrot, grated
- 2 medium zucchini, grated
- 1 tablespoon fresh rosemary, minced
- 1 tablespoon kosher salt (and more for sprinkling on after cooking)
- 2 tablespoons olive oil (and more for frying)

INSTRUCTIONS

Prep: Wipe or spray a 9 x 13" baking dish with olive oil.

1. Combine flour, water, onion, carrot, zucchini, rosemary, salt and olive oil in a medium saucepan. Heat over medium heat, stirring until mixture is very thick, for approx. 8–10 minutes.
2. When the mixture is almost too thick to stir, pour into baking dish and spread it out evenly. Mixture will set up quickly.
3. Place baking dish in the fridge. Remove after 2 hours and turn out onto a cutting board to cut into 2" long finger shapes.
4. Heat about ¾" of olive oil at medium high heat in a large frypan. Fry several pieces of panelle in the pan at a time – try not to overcrowd. Fry until golden brown; flip and brown the other side.
5. Remove cooked panelle and drain on paper towels. Sprinkle with salt while they are hot.

Serve immediately.

APPETIZERS & SNACKS

Think Outside the Box Zucchini Nachos

Here's a healthy twist to a time-tested recipe that is sure to please everyone. The only chips used in this recipe are zucchini chips.

If you are a nachos purist, consider this recipe an adventure. Take the challenge to broaden your culinary taste buds. You'll be glad you did.

And if you HAVE to, you can add a basket of tortilla chips on the side to scoop up this vegetable goodness.

INGREDIENTS

- 1 medium zucchini, sliced into rounds about ¼" thick
- 1 cup cheddar cheese, shredded
- ½ can black beans, rinsed and drained
- 1 medium tomato, chopped
- ½ large avocado, chopped
- ¼ cup red onion, chopped (can substitute green onions)
- 2 generous teaspoons fresh cilantro, finely chopped
- Juice from one lime (or lemon)
- Olive oil for brushing on zucchini rounds
- Salt and pepper to taste

INSTRUCTIONS

1. Brush zucchini rounds with olive oil, and season with salt and pepper.
2. Cook zucchini on the stovetop in a cast iron pan (medium flame for about 5 minutes), in the oven on a baking sheet (350°F for about 8–10 minutes), or on the BBQ (medium flame for about 5 minutes) until crisp.
3. Remove zucchini from the pan or grill and place on a platter. Sprinkle cheese on top of warm zucchini.
4. Layer vegetables and black beans over zucchini and season with lemon or lime juice and more salt and pepper if needed.

☞ **Note:** You can cook the zucchini chips longer and turn them into crisp chips if you prefer. The recipe for how to make crisp zucchini chips is next.

APPETIZERS & SNACKS

Crisp Zucchini Chips

Making zucchini chips is so easy that there really isn't a recipe as such.

Slice zucchini crosswise in thinnish pieces. Try to cut them the same thickness so they cook evenly. I cut them with a knife or kitchen mandolin.

☞ Option: Brush zucchini pieces with olive oil. I've made these chips both ways, with and without olive oil. They come out great either way.

Season with salt and pepper.

☞ Option: Sprinkle with parmesan cheese or other Italian cheese of your choice.

Bake in a 375°F oven for about 20 minutes or until lightly browned.

☞ Option: Dehydrate the chips for a crisp snack or to use for dipping.

Baba Ganoush

Tromboncino, also known as zucchetta (in Italian), is associated with summer squash, some equate it to zucchini. It is thought to originate from Liguria, a coastal region in northwest Italy.

I've had a fascination with this squash for years. I saw them in Sicily many years ago and was struck by their odd shape and large size. (Squash in bottom left of the picture.) I didn't think they would grow in Portland, Oregon, but to my delight, I was successful in growing a crop of them one summer.

What can you do with a tromboncino squash? Use it in about any way you would a summer squash or zucchini. For something different, I tried this recipe.

INGREDIENTS

- 4 whole zucchini or 1 large tromboncino
- ¼ cup tahini
- 2 garlic cloves, finely grated
- ½ teaspoon paprika
- Pinch of cayenne
- zest and juice of ½ lemon

GARNISH

- Hazelnuts, roasted and chopped
- Fresh mint, chopped
- Pinch of paprika
- Drizzle of olive oil

INSTRUCTIONS

1. Using a hot grill (I used our BBQ grill for added smoky flavor), cook the squash until all sides are blackened. Use tongs to turn it every so often.
2. Once done, remove and place in a bowl. Cover with foil and allow to cool until easy to handle or room temperature.
3. When cooled, carefully remove all the outer charred skin, leaving the soft flesh.
4. Mix squash flesh with tahini, garlic, lemon zest and juice, and spices. Don't over-mix or it will get watery.
5. Pour mixture onto a shallow bowl and garnish with mint, spices, chopped nuts and a good drizzle of olive oil.

APPETIZERS & SNACKS

Fruit Leather

Making fruit leather took me back a few years to when my children were young. I used to make them fruit roll-ups (as they were called at the time). There always seemed to be a batch in the dehydrator or oven.

Life can be a distraction when making a food item that requires a long cooking time. There was more than once that I turned the fruit leather into fruit candy, bark, or brittle when I left it in the oven too long. Feel free to test that result if you wish. It is actually a good outcome to a cooking mistake. I've made enough cooking mistakes to know that for a fact!

What excited me about this recipe is that it uses 20 cups of zucchini. Halleluiah! That seven-pound zucchini that had been sitting on my counter for weeks now had a destination.

The biggest warning I can give you about this recipe is drain and strain ingredients well. The first two batches I made were too wet and didn't turn into the leather consistency I expected. I dehydrated those batches a bit longer and ended up with fruit bark of sorts. Batch three came out great – just like I remembered the fruit roll-ups of yesteryear.

INGREDIENTS

- 20 cups zucchini, peeled and diced small (yielded from approximately 10 pounds zucchini)
- 64 ounces of 100% fruit juice (any flavor works)
- 3–4 tablespoons honey
- 4 cups fresh or frozen fruit (berries, cherries, apples, or your favorite)

INSTRUCTIONS

Prep: Prepare dehydrator trays or baking sheets with Silpat® sheets or parchment paper.

1. Place diced zucchini in a large pot on the stove. Pour juice over zucchini to cover pieces. Some pieces may float to the top – it's okay. You may not need the full 64 ounces of fruit juice. If so, pour yourself a glass to enjoy while cooking!
2. Heat pot to boiling and continue to boil until the zucchini are translucent. They may be discolored depending on the juice you are using.
3. Scoop zucchini out of the pot and drain any liquid juices through a strainer.
4. Batch process zucchini in the food processor blending 5 cups of zucchini, 1 cup of fruit and 1 tablespoon of honey at a time until smooth. (Repeat until all ingredients are used and blended.)
5. Strain mixture again to get out excess juices, then pour pulp onto baking sheets or dehydrator trays and smooth out evenly.
6. Dehydrate at 140°F until dry (about 12 hours). Check periodically to make sure the consistency is not becoming too brittle.
7. Once dried, remove from the dehydrator or oven, cut into strips and roll in parchment paper. Store in the fridge.

☞ **Note:** I used cranberry pomegranate juice. Fruit used was a combination of grapes and cherries. Make this with your favorite juice and fruit combination.

Soups & Sauce

Zoup

Soup in Italian is called zuppa. And I'll bet you think I was trying to Italianize the title of this recipe using a "Z" instead of "S" for the word soup. Ah, no. The "Z" is for zucchini. But you knew that, right?

I just love throwing a bunch of ingredients into a crockpot and letting them simmer the day away, filling the house with lip-smacking aromas. This recipe delivers on both fragrance and flavor!

Serve hot or cold.

INGREDIENTS

- 5 cups zucchini (skin on), chopped
- 2 shallots, chopped (see note below)
- ¼ red onion, chopped (see note below)
- 3 garlic cloves, finely chopped
- 1–2 poblano chilies, chopped (or a jalapeño pepper if you like spicy), seeds, stems, and ribs removed
- 1½ cups day-old bread, cubed
- 4 cups chicken broth (can substitute vegetable broth)
- 1 cup white wine

- 1 sprig fresh oregano, chopped (remove leaves from stem)
- 3–4 fresh basil leaves, chopped
- 1 sprig fresh thyme, chopped (remove leaves from stem)
- 2–3 tablespoons cream
- 1 teaspoon lemon juice
- Olive oil (enough to swirl the pan a few times around)
- Dash garlic herb blend seasoning
- Salt & pepper to taste
- Option: ½ cup fresh cilantro or parsley, chopped

GARNISH

- 1 tablespoon parmesan, grated
- 1 piece of bacon (turkey or regular), cooked crisp and chopped

INSTRUCTIONS

Prep: Heat the olive oil in a large pot over medium-high heat.

1. Add the onion and pepper and sauté for 4–5 minutes until the onions are translucent.
2. Add the garlic and zucchini. Sauté for another 3–4 minutes, stirring often. Sprinkle with salt.
3. Pour broth, bread and wine into pan, and bring to a simmer. Reduce heat and simmer gently for 30 minutes.
4. Add cream, and sprinkle herbs (basil, oregano, thyme) over soup. Simmer another 5 minutes. Remove from heat.
5. Add the lemon juice, salt, and pepper to taste, and cilantro or parsley (if using).
6. Purée in a blender or food processor until smooth, working in batches if necessary. (I used an immersion blender with ingredients in the cooking pot.)

☞ **Note:** Shallots and red onion combined should equal about 1 cup.

Vegetable Soup With Pizzazz

I'm getting on my Soup Box to talk about this scrumptious vegetable soup.

- It's uber healthy for starters.
- It's an easy way to use up the garden vegetable surplus (has reality hit yet that you planted one too many zucchini plants this year?).
- It can be adapted to suit a vegetarian or vegan and is gluten-free.
- It's a do-ahead meal that freezes well.
- It makes an abundant amount so you won't have to be a Soup Nazi when doling it out.
- It's yummy served hot or cold.

Well, are those enough reasons to try it?

INGREDIENTS

- 1 small onion, diced
- 2 to 3 cloves garlic, minced
- 1 cup diced carrots
- 1 cup green beans, cut into 1" pieces
- 2 whole bell peppers, chopped (red, yellow or green, or combination)
- 1 can (28 oz) regular or low sodium diced tomatoes (substitute same amount of tomatoes from the garden if abundant; whirl some in the blender to create some sauce)
- 4–6 cups beef, chicken or vegetable broth (I used only 4 cups to make a slightly thicker base)
- 2 tablespoons tomato paste
- 2 bay leaves
- ½ teaspoon each thyme & basil (or ½ to 1 tablespoon of chopped fresh thyme & basil each)
- Pepper to taste
- 2 cups chopped or julienned eggplant
- 2 cups sliced or julienned zucchini
- 4 cups spinach (or substitute cabbage if you prefer)

OPTIONAL

- ½ to 1 cup fava beans (steamed and removed from casings)
- 2 links cooked and sliced Italian sausage

INSTRUCTIONS

1. In a large pot cook sausage if using. Drain most of the drippings, leaving a little in the pan. Remove sausage and set aside. (For vegetarians, eliminate sausage and use a scant amount of olive oil instead.)
2. Sauté the carrots, green beans, onion and garlic over medium heat for about 5 minutes.
3. Stir in bell peppers, tomatoes, broth, tomato paste, bay leaves and seasonings. Simmer another 6–8 minutes.
4. Add in zucchini and eggplant. Simmer for a few minutes more.
5. Drop spinach into simmering pot of vegetables to wilt.
6. If adding optional fava beans and/or Italian sausage, do so at this point.
7. Remove bay leaves before serving.

Sprinkle with grated parmesan cheese and serve with crusty bread if desired.

Minestrone
Multivitamin in a Bowl of Goodness

Minestrone is one of the soup staples in Italian families. The word originated from minestra, which means to dish up or serve. It is considered a "big soup" and is actually a large vegetable soup that reflects both seasonal and regional variations. There is no set recipe for minestrone.

Due to its unique origins and the absence of one traditional recipe, a bowl of minestrone can vary quite a bit from region to region in Italy depending on traditional ingredients, and most importantly, the season. The common ingredients include onions, celery, carrots, tomatoes, and beans. This soup is often enriched with pasta or rice, and may or may not include meat.

The website Italian Food Forever explains:

The regional differences within Italy are reflected in the various minestrone recipes found there. In Liguria, fresh herbs are always used to season the soup whereas further south, a parmesan or pork rind is considered essential for developing good flavor. In the northern regions such as Piedmont or Lombardy, rice is most commonly used as a thickener while bread may be used in Tuscany, and pasta used further south. It also seems the further south you go in Italy the heartier and more full-bodied the ingredients that are being used are; including more tomatoes, garlic, wine, and even beef broth or bones for flavor.

Now I understand why my family (from southern Italy and Sicily) always made minestrone with healthy portions of garlic, tomatoes, wine, and pasta.

When my Italian grandparents lived with us, they would make this soup at the end of the week, using whatever vegetables were left in the garden or fridge. It never came out the same twice, but always had a familiar and robust flavor.

A note from Deborah Mele at Italian Food Forever says it all: "Minestrone to me is like a multivitamin in a bowl of goodness and should be enjoyed year round."

INGREDIENTS

- 8 ounces dried borlotti beans
- 8 ounces dried scarlet runner beans (see Scarlet Runner Beans in the Tips)
- 3 tablespoons butter
- 1–2 tablespoons olive oil
- 2 cloves of garlic; chop or leave whole
- 1 medium onion, finely chopped
- 3 tablespoons parsley, finely chopped
- 2 sage leaves, chopped
- 4 slices of pancetta, cubed (can substitute with bacon or eliminate if vegetarian)
- 2 celery stalks, chopped (I also include the leafy tops)
- 2 carrots, sliced
- 3 russet potatoes, medium size, peeled, quartered. Potatoes will break up further as they cook in soup.
- 1 teaspoon tomato paste
- 14.5-ounce can chopped tomatoes (include liquid from can)
- 8 basil leaves (can substitute 1½ teaspoons dried basil)
- 6 cups stock, vegetable and/or chicken (I use a combination of homemade vegetable bouillon [see Tips for recipe resource] and either homemade chicken stock or canned chicken stock to equal 6 cups)
- ½ to 1 cup red wine (I don't measure – I just pour)
- 1 to 2 zucchini, diced into bite-sized pieces (or vegetables of your choice)
- 5 ounces small pasta (ditalini, small shells, or other small pasta)

GARNISH

Zesto & grated parmesan cheese (see Condiments for Zesto recipe)

INSTRUCTIONS

1. Soak dried beans overnight in a large bowl covered with water.
2. Melt butter in a large saucepan and add olive oil, onion, garlic, parsley, sage, and pancetta.
3. Cook over low heat for about 10 minutes stirring occasionally until onions are soft golden brown.
4. Add celery, carrots and potatoes to the pan, cooking an additional 5 minutes.
5. Stir in tomato paste, tomatoes, basil, and drained beans.
6. Season with salt and pepper.
7. Add stock and wine, and slowly bring to a boil.
8. Cover and simmer on low for 2 hours.
9. Add zucchini and pasta at this point.
10. Simmer until pasta is al dente (about another 15–20 minutes)
11. After soup is ladled into bowls, put a dollop of zesto (or pesto) and shaved parmesan cheese on top.

☞ **Note:** Feel free to substitute your favorite beans, or seasonal vegetables. I use fresh tomatoes when available or frozen from summer season. I sometimes add sausage if I want it to be a heartier soup. If fresh ingredients aren't available, canned peas and green beans are good additions.

Zucchini Corn Chowder

Searching for a hearty soup to make? Zucchini corn chowder is a perfect choice, whether it's the end of summer, or there's a chill in the air signaling fall, a frosty winter night or a cool spring evening.

I especially like to make this soup at the end of summer with the last of the corn and zucchini harvest. My friend and I go out to a local farm and buy bushels of corn to process and freeze at the end of summer for the year. This soup is one we make as a reward for all our hard work.

INGREDIENTS

- 3 tablespoons butter
- 1¼ cups onion, diced
- ¾ cup carrots, diced
- ½ cup celery, diced
- 1½ tablespoons garlic, minced
- 1 jalapeño, diced (remove seeds/ribs)
- 1 pound red potatoes, peeled and diced (or potato of your choice)
- 3 cups chicken broth (see note)
- 1 cup vegetable broth (see note)
- 1 bay leaf
- ¼ teaspoon dried thyme (or 2 sprigs fresh thyme)
- 1½ cups zucchini, diced (about 1 large)
- 1½ cups corn kernels (frozen or sliced off the cob)
- 1 cup half-and-half (or cream)
- Salt and pepper to taste
- Optional: shake or two of garlic herb blend seasoning
- Garnish with fresh parsley

INSTRUCTIONS

1. In a large pan, melt butter over medium heat. Add onions, carrots and celery, and cook until the vegetables are softened.
2. Add garlic, jalapeños and potatoes, and cook for 3–4 minutes, stirring constantly to prevent sticking.
3. Pour the broth into the pan along with bay leaf and thyme. Bring to a boil, cover, lower heat and simmer for 8–10 minutes or until potatoes are partially cooked.
4. Combine zucchini and corn kernels into the pot and continue cooking until potatoes are cooked through. (Check by piercing potato with a fork.)
5. Remove the bay leaf before transferring approximately 2–3 cups of soup into a blender or food processor and process until smooth. (You can blend the entire soup if you want a smoother texture.)
6. Pour blended mixture back into the pot with the rest of the soup ingredients. Add half-and-half (or cream) and gently simmer to warm.

☞ **Note:** I use my homemade vegetable bouillon (see Tips for recipe resource) to create a cup of vegetable broth. You can also substitute 4 cups of just chicken broth (eliminating the vegetable broth) or 4 cups of vegetable broth only for a vegetarian version.

Chili

When it's chilly outside I like to make some chili! (A play on words for sure.) This recipe is one that I've tweaked over time, adding garden ingredients when available. It makes a big batch and freezes nicely.

Cinnamon helps tone down the chili if it is too hot for your taste buds. I use a few dashes of it, just because I like the added flavor of this secret ingredient.

Try different types of tomatoes for a flavor boost. Sometimes I substitute Mexican stewed tomatoes as one part of the tomato mixture. There are so many variations of chili you could make with this recipe!

INGREDIENTS

- 1 pound ground beef or turkey (eliminate beef or turkey for vegetarian version)
- 1 medium onion, diced
- 2 ribs celery, finely diced
- 1 medium to large carrot, shredded
- 2 cloves garlic, minced
- 1 cup zucchini, cubed
- 1 jalapeño pepper, seeded and minced
- 28-ounce can crushed tomatoes (undrained) or use 14.5-ounce can crushed or diced tomatoes (undrained) and equal amount of diced fresh tomatoes if you prefer
- 1 cup to 1 can beef broth
- 8-ounce can tomato sauce
- 30-ounce can kidney beans or 14.5-ounce can kidney beans (rinsed and drained) and equal amount of another bean such as black beans or scarlet runner beans (see note)
- 2 tablespoons chili powder
- 2 teaspoons ground cumin
- 1 teaspoon dried oregano (or for fresh oregano, double amount)
- 2 bay leaves
- ½ teaspoon salt
- Generous sprinkle of cinnamon (optional)
- Dash of cocoa powder (optional)
- Olive oil

INSTRUCTIONS

1. Drizzle olive oil in a frypan and sauté onions and celery. Add carrots and garlic for about a minute before removing all ingredients. Set aside.
2. Break up ground meat into pieces and add to frypan to cook for a few minutes. Drain.
3. In a large saucepot or Dutch oven add all ingredients and spices.
4. Bring to a boil and then reduce heat to simmer for about an hour.
5. Sprinkle chili with a dash of cinnamon and/or cocoa when almost finished cooking.

☞ **Note:** We grow scarlet runner beans in our garden, and I substitute them for half the beans used in this recipe. I cook them in beer to soften before adding them to the chili mixture. However, if you don't have scarlet runner beans, use the favorite hearty beans of your choice.

Ciambotta or Giambotta

Ciambotta or giambotta is known as minestre, which is somewhere between a thick soup and stew. It is popular in southern Italy and differs in spelling from region to region.

There are many variations of this stew, and all feature summer vegetables such as zucchini, bell peppers, potatoes, onions, tomatoes, garlic and basil, and use olive oil. It's a very flexible dish and can be served as a stand-alone vegetarian meal, or as a side dish to grilled meats and chicken.

INGREDIENTS

- ¼ cup green onion, chopped
- ¾ cup red onion, chopped
- 2 cloves of garlic, minced
- ½ cup red bell pepper, chopped
- 1 heaping cup red potatoes (or potato of your choice), peeled and cut (about 1 good sized potato)
- 2 cups zucchini chopped
- 1½ cups tomatoes, chopped
- ¼ cup cherry tomatoes, sliced in half
- ¾ to 1 cup green beans, cut into 1" pieces and flash cooked
- 1 tablespoon tomato paste
- ¼ cup wine (white or red) or substitute water instead of wine
- Salt and pepper to taste
- 1 teaspoon fresh basil, chopped
- 1 teaspoon fresh parsley, chopped
- 1 tablespoon olive oil
- Grated pecorino romano cheese to sprinkle on top of stew when done.

INSTRUCTIONS

Prep: In a large pot preheat the olive oil over medium heat.

1. Add onions, garlic, bell pepper, potatoes, zucchini and tomatoes to the pot. Season with salt and pepper to taste.
2. Sauté vegetables for about 5–7 minutes or until they start to brown.
3. Add the wine (or water) and tomato paste to the pot, cover and reduce the heat to medium low.
4. Simmer for about 25–30 minutes or until the veggies are cooked. Add green beans about the last 15 minutes of simmer to warm up in the stew.
5. During the last 5 minutes or so of cooking, remove the lid and add basil and parsley. Adjust seasoning to your taste.

Sprinkle pecorino romano cheese over the top of the stew and serve with a chunk of Italian bread.

Zucchini Pasta Sauce

Zucchini makes a wonderful pasta sauce, thick and full of flavor. I like a chucky sauce with certain pastas and this sauce never disappoints. Whether you are using garden tomatoes or canned, it comes out perfect every time!

INGREDIENTS

- 2 tablespoons butter
- 2 tablespoons olive oil
- 1¼ to 1½ cups onion, chopped (approximately 1 medium onion)
- 6 cups tomatoes, chopped (combination of San Marzano, beefsteak, and cherry tomatoes) about 2 pounds
- 2 cups zucchini, chopped small (about 1 pound)
- 3 cloves of garlic, minced
- 1 tablespoon fresh oregano, chopped
- 1½ teaspoons fresh basil, chopped
- ½ teaspoon salt
- ¼ teaspoon pepper
- ½ cup red wine
- 1 tablespoon tomato paste
- Parmigiano-Reggiano cheese, grated

INSTRUCTIONS

1. Melt butter and warm olive oil together in a large pot.
2. Sauté onions in the butter and oil until translucent.
3. Stir in tomatoes, zucchini, garlic, oregano, basil, salt and pepper. Bring to a boil.
4. Reduce heat and simmer half covered for about an hour.
5. Add wine and tomato paste to the pot. Cook for another one-half hour uncovered.
6. Serve as is (sauce will be chunky) or use an immersion blender to purée the sauce.

Serve with spaghetti of your choice or polenta. Sprinkle Parmigiano-Reggiano cheese on top.

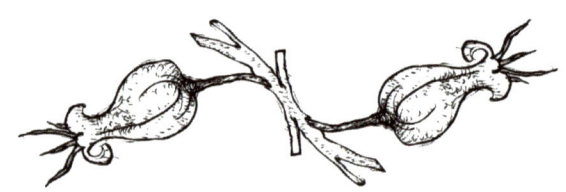

Salads

Garden Vegetable Potato Salad

This is not your traditional potato salad recipe. It's a robust potato salad using extra vegetables to fill out flavors. Its use of potatoes almost reminds me of a German potato salad, with cauliflower and zucchini blending into the recipe nicely in the background, keeping the potato the main flavor.

☞ **Note:** The dressing for this recipe makes more than is needed for this salad – at least I think so. The leftover dressing is great drizzled over barbecued fish, chicken or meat.

INGREDIENTS

- 2 pounds red potatoes, cut into 1" chunks
- Kosher salt
- ¼ cup plus 1 tablespoon olive oil
- Freshly ground black pepper
- 1 shallot, thinly sliced
- 1 cup scallion, thinly sliced
- 1 red jalapeño, thinly sliced and chopped
- 2 zucchini or yellow squash (about 1 pound), cut into 1" pieces
- 1 cup shredded cauliflower (optional)
- 1 clove garlic, minced
- Basil leaves, fresh (chiffonade or thinly sliced – see Chiffonade in Tips for chiffonade cutting tip)
- 1 large egg yolk – separated from white
- ¼ cup apple cider vinegar
- 1½ tablespoons whole grain Dijon mustard

INSTRUCTIONS

1. Cook potatoes in salted boiling water until tender when pierced (not mushy), about 12–15 minutes. Drain; set aside.
2. In a large skillet, heat 1 tablespoon olive oil over medium-high heat.
3. Add shallot, scallion and jalapeño. Cook, stirring occasionally, until shallot is soft and fragrant.
4. Add squash and cook, stirring occasionally, until crisp tender – not mushy.
5. Add cauliflower and garlic, combine with veggies in the pan and cook for another 1-2 minutes.
6. Combine potatoes, squash mixture, and basil in a large bowl.
7. Drizzle with a little Dijon dressing (see below) and toss to coat. Add more dressing if needed to moisten vegetables.
8. Season with salt and pepper.

DRESSING

1. Whisk egg yolk, vinegar and Dijon mustard in a small bowl until thoroughly combined. (Acid in vinegar "cooks" the yolk.)
2. Slowly add reserved ¼ cup oil, whisking until well emulsified.
3. Season to taste with salt and pepper; set aside.

Serve potato salad cold or warm.

Mediterranean Pasta Salad

This easy pasta salad can be put together in a matter of minutes. Pasta salad does not mean you have to use small pasta like bow tie or elbow; you can use spaghetti. I used spaghetti left over from dinner for this recipe, but if you want/need to cook spaghetti for this salad and don't want long strands, chop or snap the pasta into small pieces before you cook them.

You can add more vegetables than listed in this recipe; most are likely to work well in this salad (for example: broccoli or cauliflower) – I know zucchini does!

INGREDIENTS

- 6–8 ounces pasta
- 2 tablespoons olive oil
- ½ pound fresh green beans, ends snipped off
- ½ to 1 cup zucchini, fresh, uncooked, chopped
- 15 cherry tomatoes, halved (or more if you like tomatoes)
- 2 tablespoons red onion, chopped fine
- ¼ cup pitted kalamata olives, cut in half
- 8 fresh basil leaves (if larger leaves, cut down to 4 leaves), chiffonade or thinly sliced (see Chiffonade in Tips for chiffonade cutting tip)
- Zest and juice of 1 lemon
- Dash garlic blend seasoning
- 1 teaspoon sea salt (or more per your taste)
- Freshly ground black pepper per your taste

OPTIONAL
- Drizzle of balsamic vinegar
- Parmesan cheese

INSTRUCTIONS

1. Cook pasta according to directions on the package, and drain well. (Or if you're Italian, you know the drill with fresh pasta, right?)
2. In a medium bowl, toss the cooked pasta with the olive oil.
3. Bring 4 cups of salted water to a boil to blanch the green beans. Have a bowl of ice water ready for green bean bath. Submerge green beans in the ice water to stop cooking. Drain well and cut into bite-size pieces.
4. Stir the beans, zucchini, tomatoes, onion, olives, basil, lemon zest, lemon juice, salt and pepper into the bowl of pasta. Adjust the seasonings to taste, and serve.

☞ **Option: Sprinkle parmesan cheese over salad and drizzle thinly with balsamic vinegar.**

Vegetable Slaw Salad

Do you ever wonder what to do with the vegetables that are left over from a vegetable platter? After hosting an event, I had a few veggies left over. What I realized is that using the ingredients from a vegetable platter made making this salad so much easier because half the prep work was done.

The original vegetable platter that I made, mostly of vegetables from our garden, consisted of sugar snap peas, zucchini, and broccoli, along with purchased carrots and jicama. You could create a similar salad using the leftovers from any store-bought variety of vegetable platter.

Don't worry about chopping all ingredients the same size. I chopped the jicama much smaller than the broccoli. I just wanted a hint of crunch from the jicama and to feature more flavor from the broccoli.

So let's chop a few vegetables and enjoy!

INGREDIENTS

2½ cups broccoli, chopped
½ to ¾ cup carrots, chopped
1 cup zucchini, chopped
1 cup snap peas, cut bite size
¼ cup jicama, chopped fine

¼ cup red onion, chopped
¼ cup sunflower seeds
⅓ cup raisins or Craisins®
Salt and pepper to taste

DRESSING

⅓ cup mayonnaise
1 teaspoon vinegar

1–2 tablespoons milk for thinning (only use if dressing mixture is too thick)
Option: ⅓ cup Miracle Whip (delete vinegar if using)

INSTRUCTIONS

1. Combine all the salad ingredients except sunflower seeds and raisins/Craisins® in a large bowl.
2. Mix dressing in a separate bowl to a thickish consistency.
3. Pour dressing over vegetable mixture and toss well.
4. Chill for about 1 hour. Sprinkle sunflower seeds and raisins or Craisins® on the salad before serving.

☞ **Note:** I used Miracle Whip and no vinegar. Also, I did not need to thin the dressing. Be careful if you do because it will thin down as it marries with the vegetables.

Quinoa Vegetable Salad

How often have you heard this line repeated from the movie *When Harry Met Sally:* "I'll have what she's having"? All who enjoyed the movie remember the famous scene where this line originated.

This quinoa vegetable salad is simple and easy to make, as well as nutritious and tasty. And it is sure to spark the line "I'll have what he/she's having" when any vegetable lover spots it on your plate. You may even convert a few people to enjoy vegetables just a little more.

INGREDIENTS

- 2 cups fat-free reduced-sodium chicken broth (for a vegetarian option, substitute same quantity of vegetable broth)
- 1 cup quinoa, uncooked
- 2 cups fresh spinach, tightly packed, chopped
- 2 carrots, coarsely shredded
- 1 small zucchini, coarsely shredded
- 1 medium tomato, chopped
- 1–2 green onions, chopped
- 1 clove garlic, minced
- 1–2 leaves fresh basil chiffonade cut (see Chiffonade in Tips for chiffonade cutting tip)
- 2–3 tablespoons balsamic vinegar and dash of good olive oil (or use a vinaigrette dressing if you prefer)
- ¼ cup feta cheese, crumbled

INSTRUCTIONS

1. Bring broth and quinoa to boil in saucepan on high heat; simmer on medium-low heat 15 minutes or until liquid is absorbed. Cool before adding into salad ingredients.
2. Mix cooled quinoa with spinach, carrots, zucchini, green onions, and garlic in large bowl.
3. Add tomatoes, basil, and cheese to quinoa salad mixture.

Stir in dressing and serve.

Grilled Corn, Cucumber & Tomato Salad

Most salads are at their best in summer when you can take advantage of the in-season vegetables. You'll enjoy this salad any time of year by switching out fresh corn on the cob for canned or frozen, or substituting another in-season vegetable. Experiment with your vegetable favorites to create your own customized dish!

The Honey Lime Dressing pairs with a lot of salad ingredients nicely and can be used with any type of salad any time of year.

Serves 4.

INGREDIENTS

1 corn on the cob

1½ cups cherry tomatoes, halved

1 cup cucumber, cubed

1 cup zucchini, cubed

2 tablespoons red onion, diced

DRESSING

Juice from 1 lemon

1 tablespoon honey

2 tablespoons oil (olive or canola)

2 teaspoons balsamic vinegar

1 garlic clove, minced

Dash of cayenne pepper

Salt & pepper

GARNISH

1–2 tablespoons blue cheese (options: feta or goat cheese)

INSTRUCTIONS

1. Grill the corn on the BBQ to a slight char. When cooled, shave the kernels off the cob. Set aside.
2. In a medium-sized bowl combine tomatoes, cucumber, zucchini, red onion, and cooled corn kernels.
3. Mix together dressing ingredients. Pour over salad mixture, being careful to watch the saturation of the vegetables. I slowly drip the dressing over the vegetables, stir, and then add more dressing as necessary. You don't want to drown the vegetables, just kiss them with a little moisture.
4. Crumble your cheese of choice over the salad just before serving.

☞ Option: serve over lettuce for a meal, or as a side dish.

Zucchini and Veggie Stir-Fry Salad

One of my favorite vegetable dishes! It can be eaten cold as a salad, as a side dish, and even as a warm meatless lunch or dinner. I grow all of the ingredients in the spring and summer, even the garlic, onions, and pepperoncini. However, all ingredients are available at the grocery store or farmer's market if you don't have your own garden. Make sure you wash all the vegetables before chopping them, whether they come from a store, farmer's market or garden.

The exact vegetables may vary over the summer and throughout the year – spring sugar snap peas being replaced by pole beans or other late summer vegetables – cooked or uncooked. Be creative with the ingredients you favor most.

INGREDIENTS

- ½ white onion, chopped (can substitute red onion)
- 2 small zucchini, chopped (leave skin on)
- 1 cup green beans (preferably fresh and parboiled), cut into bite-sized pieces
- 1 cup sugar snap peas, cut into bite-sized pieces
- 2 tomatoes, chopped
- 2–3 cloves of garlic, finely chopped
- ¼ cup roasted red peppers, chopped (jarred or fresh roasted)
- Several sprinkles of dried thyme and oregano
- Salt and pepper to taste
- Sprinkle overall with garlic herb blend seasoning
- Scant olive oil to coat sauté pan
- Drizzle of balsamic vinegar
- Sprinkle of parmesan cheese
- Optional: pepperoncini stemmed and seeded, finely chopped (for extra zing)

INSTRUCTIONS

1. Drizzle olive oil in a frypan and add onions and zucchini. Sauté for a few minutes until the onions and zucchini start to soften.
2. Add green beans and sugar snap peas, along with tomatoes and garlic. (Add more oil if needed.)
3. Once vegetables are well mixed, season with salt, pepper, garlic, and herbs.
4. If using fresh red pepper, char on stovetop and roast to soften.
5. Stir in roasted red peppers and pepperoncini (optional) until warm.
6. Remove veggies from stovetop, and plate. Add more salt and pepper if needed.
7. Sprinkle with parmesan and drizzle with balsamic vinegar.

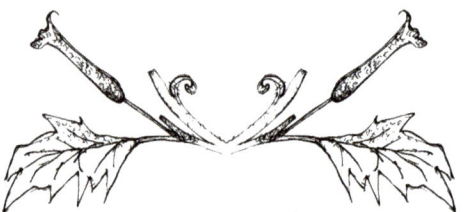

Houdini Zucchini Disguised as Lasagna

Houdini Zucchini? This recipe is so tasty, it will make your zucchini disappear!

Trying to cook gluten free, or scale back on carbs? This recipe is for you! In creating this easy vegetarian meal, I incorporated two Italian food favorites – Eggplant Parmesan and Lasagna ingredients. If you want to add meat, it's easy to include cooked ground beef, ground turkey, or Italian sausage to a couple of layers when assembling.

Serves 6–8 as a side dish, or about 4 as a main dish.

INGREDIENTS

ZUCCHINI PARMESAN

- 2 pounds zucchini (about 2 average size)
- Salt and pepper
- 3 tablespoons extra-virgin olive oil
- ½ cup freshly grated parmesan

FILLING

- 1 cup fresh ricotta cheese (see Tips for for homemade recipe resource) or use store brand
- ½ cup plain low-fat Greek yogurt
- 1–2 large cloves of garlic minced
- Small handful of Italian parsley, well chopped
- Several leaves of basil, well chopped
- Salt and pepper to taste

SAUCE

- 1 jar spaghetti sauce (your favorite store brand) or about 3 cups homemade (recipe resource for simple homemade sauce in Tips)

INSTRUCTIONS

1. Line 2 sheet pans with parchment.
2. Trim ends off zucchini and cut in half crosswise, then into lengthwise slices, about ¼ to ⅓" thick. (Cutting zucchini in half makes it easier to handle and slice lengthwise.)
3. Place zucchini slices on baking sheets in one layer. Brush both sides with olive oil and then season with salt and pepper.
4. Roast for 12 to 15 minutes in a 400°F preheated oven, until lightly browned and easily pierced with a fork.
5. Remove from oven and reduce heat to 375°F.
6. Spray oil in a lasagna dish or oblong casserole dish.
7. Spread ¼ cup tomato sauce over bottom of dish.
8. Start layers with a third of the zucchini in an even layer over tomato sauce.
9. Spoon cheese mixture over zucchini.
10. Spoon a third of remaining sauce over zucchini and sprinkle with Parmesan.
11. Repeat with 2 more layers, ending with sauce and Parmesan.
12. Bake 30 to 35 minutes, until bubbling and browned on the top and edges.

Mediterranean Pizza

Stepping away from traditional pizza toppings can be a stretch for some, but the flavors of this Mediterranean pizza are so good, it has even won over a few pepperoni pizza purists. And the bonus is that it incorporates much healthier ingredients, including zucchini of course!

INGREDIENTS

- 3 tablespoons olive oil
- 1 tablespoon butter plus 1 pat of butter to pre-cook mushrooms
- 2 cups thinly sliced yellow onion
- ½ to 1 cup thinly sliced red onion
- 1 teaspoon fresh garlic, minced
- 1–2 cups zucchini, thinly shaved
- ½ cup mushrooms, sliced
- 1 small/medium tomato, thinly sliced
- ¼ to ½ cup feta, grated
- ¼ cup kalamata olives, pitted and chopped
- Balsamic vinegar
- 3–4 tablespoons pasta sauce
- Pizza dough, purchased or homemade

INSTRUCTIONS

Prep: Preheat oven to 450°F. Heat pizza stone in oven until ready to assemble.

1. Prepare dough and roll out to fit your pizza stone or baking sheet.
2. In a frypan heat olive oil and melt 1 tablespoon butter over medium low heat.
3. Add onions to frypan and cook down until soft, then add garlic (about 10–15 minutes total to caramelize onions).
4. Option: Pre-cook mushrooms in 1 pat of butter until done. I like them crispy so I fry a little longer. If you don't like your mushrooms pre-cooked, just slice and have ready to top pizza.

ASSEMBLE PIZZA

1. Carefully spread dough out on hot stone and brush top with a thin layer of pasta sauce.
2. Layer onions and mushrooms on top, followed by tomato and zucchini. Sprinkle feta over vegetables.
3. Bake until crust is nicely browned and zucchini looks cooked (about 15–20 minutes).
4. Top with olives and drizzle with olive oil and balsamic vinegar.

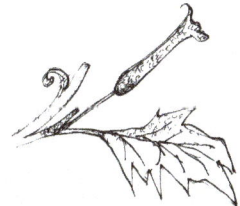

MAIN DISHES

Sicilian Caponata Marries Pasta

When we were visiting my family in Italy over 20 years ago, my aunt made a pasta dish similar to this one. We had arrived at the family house late in the afternoon (not dinner time) hungry from traveling. They were surprised to see us because they thought we were visiting them the following week.

Even though it was not really a mealtime, my aunt whipped up a simple pasta dish with sardines, peppers, onions and capers. No sauce, just olive oil drizzled over these ingredients with a few seasonings. It was amazing! She prepared and served us this dish practically before we had a chance to set our suitcases down.

I've added a few Sicilian caponata ingredients to create this wonderful pasta meal. While I may be standing in my kitchen in Oregon making this recipe, my head and heart are in Italy remembering this wonderful meal shared with my Italian family.

INGREDIENTS

- 1 16-ounce package of uncooked pasta (I used angel hair)
- ½ medium onion, chopped
- 1 medium red pepper, chopped
- 1 medium to large zucchini chopped into cubes (could substitute a combination of squashes and eggplant)
- 2 tablespoons pine nuts
- 2 tablespoons raisins
- 2 tablespoons capers
- 1 3.5-ounce can sardines in oil
- Peccorino reggiano for garnish
- Olive oil
- Salt and pepper to taste

INSTRUCTIONS

1. Drizzle olive oil in a frypan. Sauté onions, pepper and zucchini until softened.
2. Add pine nuts, raisins, and capers to the sautéed vegetables and cook for another minute or two.
3. Break up the sardines with your fingers or a spoon and add (along with the oil from the sardine tin) to the frypan and mix with vegetables. (You can break up the sardines into chunks or finely mash them – whatever you prefer.)
4. Cook pasta in a large pot of generously salted boiling water until just shy of al dente. (It will continue to cook when sautéed with vegetables.)
5. Drain and add cooked pasta into vegetables and sauté until all ingredients are combined.
6. Season with salt and pepper and add more olive oil if needed.

Sprinkle with cheese and serve.

MAIN DISHES

Chicken Stir-Fry

Stir-fry recipes are so easy and require little more effort than cutting up vegetables, sautéing them in a little oil, and adding chunked meat, fish, or chicken.

You can chop up the vegetables in about any shape you wish. I was having fun experimenting with my mandolin and julienned the zucchini, but it is not necessary.

INGREDIENTS

- 2 cups chicken, cut into bite-sized pieces
- 1 zucchini, julienned or chopped into bite-sized pieces
- ¼ cup peas (fresh or frozen)
- 1 handful of sugar snap peas or green beans (about 1 cup)
- 2 carrots, cut into bite-sized pieces or julienned
- 1 stalk celery, chopped into small pieces
- ½ cup onion (red or white), chopped fine
- ¼ cup jicama, chopped into small pieces (optional)
- 2 garlic cloves, minced
- Sesame seeds (optional)
- Canola oil swirled around pan – enough to sauté vegetables and chicken
- Few dashes of sesame oil
- Few dashes of hot pepper (Tabasco®) or Sriracha sauce (optional)
- Few dashes of soy sauce
- Few sprigs of fresh cilantro, chopped (optional)
- Salt & pepper
- Dash of garlic herb blend seasoning

INSTRUCTIONS

1. Sauté chicken in canola oil until almost done.
2. Add vegetables to the pan – along with a few dashes of sesame oil.
3. Cook for a few minutes on medium to high heat (don't let vegetables get soggy or overcooked) - stir quickly around the pan so vegetables are covered in the oils.
4. Season with salt and pepper and garlic herb blend. If using, add cilantro at this time.

☞ **Note:** Serve as is or over a bed of rice or pasta

Greek Turkey Burgers

Did you know you can substitute zucchini peels for spinach or kale in some recipes? Many recipes use zucchini with the peel on, so I was thinking…it's edible, why not use the peels by themselves in recipes? An opportunity presented itself for me to try this theory out.

I was in the middle of making Greek turkey burgers and realized I didn't have any spinach on hand. Not wanting to abandon the task at hand and run to the grocery store, I decided to use zucchini peels instead. So I carefully peeled a zucchini, chopped up the peels into small pieces and added them to the burger patties as I would have if it were spinach. These Greek turkey burgers turned out great!

INGREDIENTS

- 1 pound lean ground turkey
- ½ cup zucchini peels, finely chopped and squeezed dry
- 2–3 cloves garlic, minced
- ½ cup feta cheese, crumbled and/or mashed
- ½ teaspoon Worcestershire sauce
- ½ teaspoon garlic powder
- ½ teaspoon dried oregano
- ¼ teaspoon Mediterranean salt
- ¼ teaspoon freshly ground pepper

INSTRUCTIONS

1. Sauté zucchini peels in a frying pan with scant olive oil. When they start to soften, add minced garlic. Stir to keep garlic from burning. Set aside to cool.
2. Thoroughly mix ground turkey, zucchini, feta, spices and herbs in a medium bowl – using your hands if possible to get best incorporation of all ingredients.
3. Form into patties and refrigerate for 2 to 4 hours before grilling. (Or you can freeze at this point for cooking another day.)
4. Oil a grill rack for cooking on BBQ or swirl olive oil in a frypan and heat on stove before adding burgers to the pan.
5. Cook about 5 minutes per side and check for doneness by inserting a food thermometer. It should register 165°F.

Serve immediately on hamburger bun or in pita bread with tomato, lettuce, red onion, and sliced cucumber. Spreads can vary from mayonnaise to zesto, zucchini relish or zucchini spread. (See Condiments for recipes.)

Chicken Artichoke With Zucchini Ribbons

Chicken artichoke with zucchini ribbons is a recipe created by a friend and neighbor Mike. His special culinary talents are shown off when he puts recipes together, adding a little of this and a little of that. The results are always spectacular. Mike was a recipient of one of my overload zucchini and he came up with a brilliant way to use it.

INGREDIENTS

- 2 to 4 boneless, skinless chicken breasts
- 4 to 6 ounces fresh sliced mushrooms
- 1 14-ounce can of quartered artichoke hearts packed in water, drained
- ¾ cup grated or shredded parmesan cheese
- ¾ cup mayonnaise
- 4 cloves garlic, minced, divided
- 1 to 4 fresh zucchini, depending on size. One large zucchini is enough for 2 large servings
- 1 teaspoon olive oil
- Salt and pepper to taste

INSTRUCTIONS

Prep: Heat oven to 375°F. Lightly coat baking dish with oil.

1. While oven is heating, sauté mushrooms until tender.
2. Rinse chicken breasts and pat dry, arrange in cooking dish and sprinkle with salt and pepper.
3. Top chicken with sautéed mushrooms.
4. Coarsely chop artichoke hearts.
5. In a bowl, combine artichoke hearts, parmesan cheese, mayonnaise, and 2 cloves of the minced garlic.
6. Mix well and spread over the mushrooms and chicken breasts.
7. Bake uncovered for 30–35 minutes or until juices run clear.
8. While chicken is baking, prepare and sauté the zucchini ribbons.
9. After washing the zucchini, trim away both ends and using a vegetable peeler, shave the zucchini on all sides until you reach the seeds. Discard the seeded center.
10. Place shaved zucchini on a thin kitchen towel and lightly press to remove excess moisture.
11. Heat olive oil in a large skillet over medium heat.
12. Add reserved garlic and cook for about 1 minute.
13. Add zucchini ribbons and toss with tongs to coat with oil. Cook until warm and barely tender; about 5–6 minutes.
14. Sprinkle with salt and pepper.
15. Make a bed of cooked zucchini ribbons on each plate; top with a serving of the chicken bake.
16. Adjust seasonings to taste.

MAIN DISHES

Beef Enchiladas & Burrito Boats

This recipe makes two different meals using zucchini. The first recipe, Beef Enchiladas, uses thinly sliced zucchini ribbons that are overlapped to create a house for the enchilada filling. The second recipe, Burrito Boats, carves out a whole zucchini for stuffing and uses the pulp in the stuffing mix.

Cooking up 1 pound of hamburger (or ground turkey) yields enough to supply both recipes.

Beef Enchiladas

INGREDIENTS

- 1 pound ground beef
- 1 onion, chopped
- 1 tablespoon olive oil
- 1½ cups red enchilada sauce, divided
- 2 cloves garlic, minced
- 2 teaspoons chili powder
- 1 teaspoon cumin
- 1 large zucchini
- 1 cup Monterey jack cheese, shredded
- 1 cup cheddar cheese, shredded
- Salt and pepper to taste

INSTRUCTIONS

Prep: heat oven to 350°F. Spray an 8 x 8" or 7 x 10" baking pan with cooking spray.

1. Warm oil in a large frypan over medium-low heat.
2. Add onion and ground beef, cooking until beef is no longer pink. Drain excess fat.
3. Add 1 cup enchilada sauce to the skillet along with garlic, chili powder and cumin. Season meat mixture with salt and pepper and simmer 5 minutes. Set aside 1 cup of meat mixture for the Burrito Boat recipe.
4. Using a vegetable peeler or thin setting on a mandolin, cut a zucchini into thin slices lengthwise.
5. Lay 3 slices of zucchini together overlapping slightly and place 1–2 spoonfuls of beef mixture and a tablespoon of mixed cheeses on the zucchini slices.
6. Roll up filled zucchini slices and place into the baking dish. When done with all the zucchini and filling, spoon the remaining one-half cup enchilada sauce over the enchiladas and sprinkle with the remaining cheeses.
7. Bake uncovered until cheese is melted – about 20 minutes.

Burrito Boats

INGREDIENTS

- 2 zucchini, sliced lengthwise (makes 4 boats)
- 1 cup ground beef mixture from Beef Enchiladas recipe
- ½ cup cherry tomatoes, chopped
- ½ cup black or pinto beans
- ½ cup corn, fresh cut off the cob, canned, or frozen
- ½ cup Monterey jack cheese, shredded
- ½ cup cheddar cheese, shredded
- 1 tablespoon olive oil
- Salt and pepper to taste

INSTRUCTIONS

Prep: Preheat oven to 350°F. Spray a 9 x 13" baking dish with cooking oil.

1. Scoop out the insides of each zucchini half, leaving enough flesh to support stuffing mixture. Set the pulp aside.
2. Place the zucchini boats in a baking dish, drizzle with olive oil and sprinkle with salt and pepper. Cook for about 10 minutes, until zucchini is beginning to soften.
3. Drizzle a little olive oil in a skillet and warm up over medium heat. Add reserved zucchini pulp, ground beef from enchilada recipe, tomatoes, black beans, and corn. Warm together for a few minutes.
4. Spoon beef mixture into zucchini boats and top with cheeses. Bake about 15 minutes or until cheeses are melted.

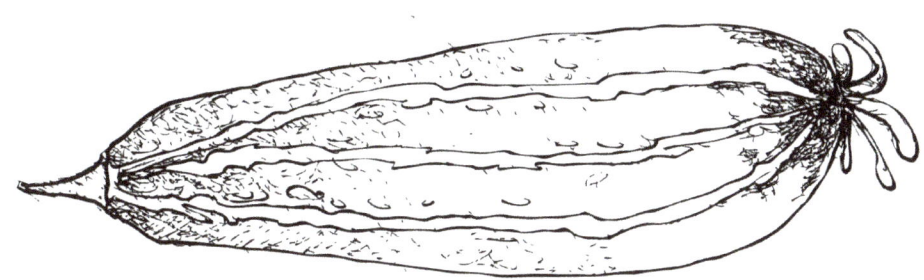

Bacon, Zucchini, & Tomato Sandwich

You don't need lettuce to make this bacon, zucchini and tomato (BZT) sandwich, although you can add it if you like. This is a quick sandwich to assemble.

Recipe makes 1 serving and is topless. Add another slice of bread if you prefer.

INGREDIENTS

- 2 large slices of zucchini
- 1–2 thin slices red onion
- 1–2 slices of bacon (options: turkey, pepper, or applewood)
- 2–3 slices tomato (just enough to cover sandwich)
- 1–2 tablespoons jack cheese shredded or sliced (option: pepper jack cheese)
- 1 slice of bread (I used Dave's Killer Bread or use your favorite)
- Drizzle of olive oil
- Option: zucchini spread (see Condiments for recipe) or mayo brushed on bread

INSTRUCTIONS

1. Toast bread and set aside.
2. In a small frypan drizzle olive oil and warm. Add zucchini slices and onion slices. Sauté until slightly softened.
3. Assemble sandwich with spread of your choice on the bread (or no spread if you prefer), layering vegetables on top of each other, ending with tomatoes on top, covered with cheese.

☞ Option: Place sandwich under the broiler for a minute to melt the cheese.

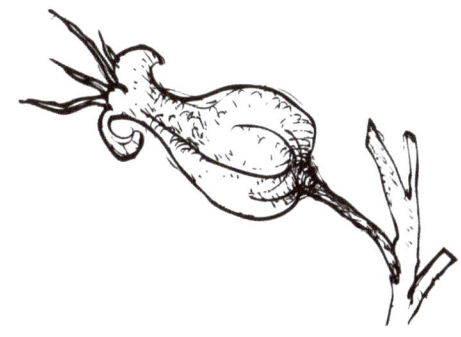

Farro Casserole

Farro is an underused grain in most U.S. households but has been eaten around the world for thousands of years. This ancient wheat grain is an excellent source of protein, fiber and nutrients like magnesium and iron. I learned how to really cook it one summer when I was visiting Vinci, Italy.

Amusing backstory to this recipe:

- I carefully sliced the zucchini with my mandolin to make precise pieces and the reality was, it didn't matter because the zucchini softened so much that I mashed it (see next point).
- I tried making zucchini rice by using a potato ricer to "rice" the cooked zucchini into the main ingredients. That didn't work. The zucchini just mushed — but the ricer did extract additional liquid.
- I had intended to use sour cream in the list of ingredients and realized when I opened the sour cream carton, I didn't have enough. I substituted fresh ricotta cheese that turned out to be a good alternative. So if you don't have ricotta you can substitute sour cream, either works.

I have to admit that this recipe was a challenge to get the ingredients and directions just the way I wanted them. In the end, everything worked out and the dish came out great. You can thank me later for making all the mistakes for you.

INGREDIENTS

- 4–4 ½ cups zucchini (about 2 pounds zucchini)
- ½ cup onion
- ¼ cup chicken stock
- 1 egg
- 1 cup farro (or brown rice)
- ¼ cup ricotta (or sour cream)
- ¼ cup plain low-fat Greek yogurt (or use ½ cup ricotta instead of ¼ Greek yogurt and ¼ ricotta)
- 3 tablespoons parmesan cheese (divided 2 tablespoons and 1 tablespoon)
- ¾ cup cheddar cheese
- Few dashes of Tabasco sauce (or hot sauce)
- ⅛ teaspoon each oregano, basil, parsley
- Generous sprinkle of garlic blend seasoning
- Salt and pepper to taste
- Option: zucchini chips (see page 31)

INSTRUCTIONS

Prep: Preheat oven to 350°F. Spray an 8 x 8" baking dish with cooking oil.

1. Combine zucchini, onion and chicken broth in a pot. Cover and bring to a boil, cooking for 20 minutes or until tender.
2. Drain liquid from zucchini mixture and mash with fork or potato masher.
3. Mix zucchini with egg, farro, ricotta, yogurt, cheddar cheese, 2 tablespoons parmesan cheese and seasonings. Pour into prepared baking dish. Top with the remainder of parmesan cheese.

☞ Option: top with zucchini chips (before baking).

Bake for 30–35 minutes or until golden brown.

MAIN DISHES

Zucchini Corn Fritters

INGREDIENTS

- 1 pound zucchini, grated (about 1½ cups after squeezing)
- 1 teaspoon salt
- 1 cup corn kernels, frozen, canned, or roasted and cut off the cob
- 4 large eggs, beaten
- ½ teaspoon dried basil
- ½ teaspoon dried oregano
- ¼ teaspoon garlic powder
- Kosher salt and freshly ground black pepper, to taste
- ¾ cup shredded cheddar cheese
- ¾ cup all-purpose flour
- 2 tablespoons olive oil
- 1 tablespoon grated onion

INSTRUCTIONS

1. Place grated zucchini in a colander over the sink. Add salt and gently toss to combine; let sit for 10 minutes. Squeeze and drain zucchini in a clean dishcloth.

2. In a large bowl, combine zucchini, corn, eggs, basil, oregano and garlic powder; season with salt and pepper to taste. Stir in cheese and flour until well combined.

3. Heat olive oil in a large skillet over medium high heat. Scoop tablespoons of batter for each fritter into the pan and cook until the underside is nicely golden brown, about 2 minutes. Flip and flatten if needed, cooking on the other side about 1–2 minutes longer.

SIDE DISHES

Squash Blossoms Stuffed With Ricotta

At one point when we first moved to Oregon from Southern California I actually had a tough time growing zucchini. The plants would generate plenty of blossoms but tamp out before the zucchini produced the vegetable. It just would not grow in the various garden spots I had planted it. I created this recipe to use the blossoms.

After ten years of experimenting every space in our small yard (I was patient), I finally found a "spot" where it now thrives year after year. Its favorite space is in the front yard in a semi-rock garden. My theory is that the rocks keep the plants warm and they just produce, produce, produce! Now I can steal enough flowers from the plants to make this recipe a few times during the growing season.

INGREDIENTS

12 to 16 zucchini flowers

1 cup fresh ricotta cheese (see Tips for recipe resource) or store brand

1 egg yolk

⅔ cup grated parmigiano reggiano divided

TOMATO DIPPING SAUCE

1 garlic clove, minced

¼ teaspoon pepper flakes or small red pepper minced

2 tablespoons olive oil

1½ pounds plum tomatoes, finely chopped

1 cup all-purpose flour

Vegetable oil for frying – generous amount

12-ounce beer, seltzer, or club soda

1 handful fresh parsley finely chopped

Kosher salt and freshly ground black pepper

½ cup water

½ teaspoon sugar

½ teaspoon salt

INSTRUCTIONS

1. Carefully open each flower (use your fingers to open up the middle). Take out pollen stem. Gently rinse the flowers – try not to damage the thin petals. Lay on a tea towel and pat dry.

2. Stir together ricotta, egg yolk, one-half of the parmesan and one-eighth teaspoon each of salt and pepper.

3. Fill a piping bag (or zipped sandwich bag with corner cut off) with the cheese mixture and pipe a tablespoon or so into each flower. You can also use a small spoon to stuff the flowers. Gently twist end of blossom to enclose filling.

4. Whisk together flour, parsley, generous pinch of salt and a few grinds of pepper. Slowly pour beer or seltzer into the mix and stir – eliminating any lumps.

5. Heat a generous amount of oil (1" or so) to 375°F in a large heavy skillet. Dip blossoms into the batter to thinly coat. Carefully add to the hot oil, fry, and flip halfway through frying until blossoms are golden and crisp – about 2 minutes. Remove and place on paper towels to drain.

6. Sprinkle with salt and pepper while hot. Serve with tomato dipping sauce.

TOMATO DIPPING SAUCE

Cook garlic and red pepper in oil in a saucepan over medium heat, stirring until garlic is slightly golden, only about 30 seconds. Add tomatoes, water, sugar and one-half teaspoon salt. Simmer uncovered, stirring occasionally until thickened, about 25–30 minutes.

Sicilian Caponata

One of my favorite experiences in Sicily was when I took a cooking class from Massimo in Taormina. His recipes were from his nonna. Nonna cooked on Sunday for the family and there were always 20 people who came to dinner. So all of Massimo's recipes made enough for 20 people. This makes sense, well maybe only to Massimo and Italians? However, that does pose a challenge if you don't have 20 people to feed when making any of Massimo's recipes.

Massimo's English was good enough for teaching his cooking classes, but his recipes showed some language discrepancies that I just adore when I read them. One of his recipes was particularly entertaining – "don't **movie** the vegetables" and "when you **finnish** every **think** chop **fin**." To be fair, if I was translating any of my recipes to Italian (with or without Google translate) they would be much funnier than this – if even comprehensible.

This recipe has been altered to serve 5 instead of 20.

INGREDIENTS

- 2 zucchini, chopped or cubed
- 2 eggplants, chopped or cubed
- 2 peppers, chopped
- 1 white onion, chopped
- 1 stalk celery, chopped
- ¼ cup olives
- 2 tablespoons capers
- ¼ cup pine nuts
- ¼ cup raisins
- 2 teaspoons sugar
- 2 teaspoons white vinegar
- Pinch of salt

INSTRUCTIONS

1. Fry zucchini, eggplant, and peppers separately in vegetable oil. This preserves the flavor of each vegetable.
2. In olive oil cook onion and celery to soft and golden.
3. Add olives, capers, pine nuts and raisins to onions and celery.
4. Add the sugar and then add vinegar. Add the zucchini and eggplant.
5. Season with salt and serve.

Can be eaten hot – room temperature is best.

Tater Zots

Kids and adults love these potato zucchini zot morsels. They just might become your preferred way of fixing potatoes and including a healthy vegetable neatly tucked inside. And it can't get much easier than two main ingredients.

INGREDIENTS

3 russet potatoes, peeled and chopped

2 zucchini (2–3 cups shredded and squeezed dry)

1 teaspoon salt (divided to sprinkle some on top)

Olive oil

INSTRUCTIONS

Prep: Preheat oven to 425°F.

1. Place potatoes in a pot, cover with water, and bring to a boil.
2. Cook for 20–30 minutes until potatoes are fork tender. Drain and cool potatoes.
3. Mash or shred cooked potatoes until they are broken up and not lumpy.
4. Combine zucchini, potatoes and salt thoroughly. Form into small cylinders and place on a parchment-lined cookie sheet. Place in the fridge for 15–20 minutes.
5. Remove from the fridge, brush zots with olive oil and sprinkle with salt before putting in the oven. Cook for 30 minutes. Flip halfway through.

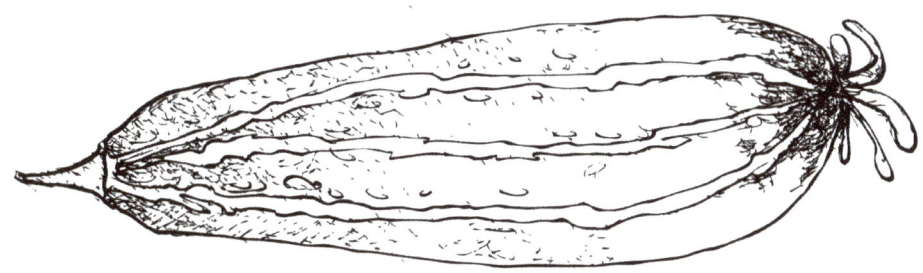

No Hassle Hasselback Zucchini

INGREDIENTS

- 1 tablespoon extra-virgin olive oil
- ½ teaspoon oregano, dried
- ½ teaspoon thyme, dried
- ¼ teaspoon garlic powder
- ¼ teaspoon salt
- ¼ teaspoon ground pepper
- 4 small zucchini (about 1 pound total)
- ½ cup shaved parmesan cheese, or your favorite (I used pecorino romano)

INSTRUCTIONS

Prep: Preheat grill to medium-high.

1. Combine oil, oregano, thyme, garlic powder, salt and pepper in a small bowl.
2. Set up two wooden spoons parallel to each other on your cutting board. Place the zucchini in between the handles of two wooden spoons. This will block the knife cuts from going all the way through the vegetable as the bottom of the zucchini will be below the wooden spoon handles. Make cuts every ½" along the zucchini, slicing almost to the bottom but not all the way through.

3. Gently fan the zucchini to open the cuts wider, and place a small piece of cheese into each cut.
4. Brush the oil mixture over the top of the zucchini.
5. Place the zucchini on a double layer of foil and grill, without turning, until browned and tender, 16 to 18 minutes.

Fifty Shades of Color in Garden Vegetables

The rich colors of ripe vegetables are so vibrant in this dish. It's a quick and easy recipe, it's vegetarian, and so versatile with ingredients (substitute in your favorites). In the summer, it's truly a garden to table meal with fifty shades of color. Well, maybe 38 or 39 shades of color, oh, who's counting anyway?

INGREDIENTS

- 1 medium sized zucchini cut into bite-sized chunks
- 1 small onion, chopped
- 1 shallot, chopped or sliced
- 3 cloves of garlic, sliced
- 2 tomatoes, chopped (San Marzano or your favorite tomato of equal amount)
- 3 sweet Italian peppers, seeded and julienned (option – leave out if you wish – Italian sweet peppers aren't hot and only add flavor)
- 1 cup green beans, blanched and cut into bite-sized pieces
- 1–2 tablespoons of fresh oregano and thyme
- Salt and pepper
- Olive oil for sautéing
- Pecorino romano cheese, shaved (a few shavings to top the vegetables)

INSTRUCTIONS

1. Blanch the green beans.
2. Add all vegetables to a frypan that has been drizzled with olive oil. (Don't add the garlic until most vegetables are softened to avoid burning it.)
3. Cook vegetables until they are done to your liking or softened but still a bit crispish.
4. Top with shavings of pecorino romano cheese and serve immediately.

SIDE DISHES

Vegetable Galette

"Mary, Mary quite contrary how does your garden grow?" With zucchini, eggplant, tomatoes, garlic, and onions? This sweet and savory recipe is perfect to use up the bountiful harvest of garden vegetables.

Slice like a pie for appetizers or dinner. Enjoy the sweet/savory flavor of this recipe – slightly sweet pie crust and savory vegetables. Makes a wonderful vegetarian meal.

INGREDIENTS

- 1 unbaked pie crust (store bought like Pillsbury® brand)
- 2 to 3 tablespoons of tomato sauce (or hummus if you prefer)
- 1 clove garlic, minced
- 1 zucchini, thinly sliced crosswise
- 1 medium eggplant, thinly sliced crosswise
- 1 to 2 beefsteak tomatoes, thinly sliced
- ½ small onion, thinly sliced (white, yellow or red)
- Kosher salt and freshly ground pepper
- Olive oil
- ¼ cup grated parmesan
- 1 heaping teaspoon fresh thyme leaves, finely chopped
- 1 heaping teaspoon fresh oregano leaves, finely chopped
- ¼ cup picante provolone cheese, grated or thinly sliced
- 1 egg
- Option: can substitute provolone for picante provolone

INSTRUCTIONS

Prep: Preheat oven to 400°F.

1. Lay the thinly sliced zucchini, eggplant, tomatoes and onion onto baking sheets lined with paper towels. Season with salt and pepper.

2. Let vegetables sit for about 20 minutes to draw out excess moisture.

3. Roll out the pie crust into a large circle until it's about ¼" thick. Transfer to a parchment paper–lined baking sheet.

4. Stir minced garlic into the tomato sauce, then spoon and spread on the center of the pie dough, leaving about a 1" border along the perimeter.

5. Arrange the vegetable slices side-by-side and overlapping, starting at the outer edge and following the perimeter of the dough. Alternate between zucchini, onions, tomatoes, and eggplant.

6. Repeat by making an inner circle of vegetables and continue until the entire pie is filled. (You may have leftover vegetables depending on how you overlap the slices.)

7. Fold the edges of the dough over the vegetables.

8. Make an egg wash by whisking an egg. Brush the egg wash onto the crust. Sprinkle parmesan, oregano, and thyme over vegetables.

9. Drizzle olive oil over vegetables before putting in the oven.

10. Bake the galette for 40 minutes, or until the crust is golden brown and the vegetables are tender.*

11. Check galette at about 35 minutes. Pierce the vegetables with a fork to see if they are cooked. If so remove from oven. If not, let it remain in the oven the full 40 minutes or more to thoroughly cook the vegetables.*

12. Once the galette is removed from the oven, sprinkle provolone on top. The hot vegetables will easily melt the cheese.

Let it rest for 5–10 minutes before slicing.

☞ **Tip**: Evenly and thinly slice the vegetables (or use a mandolin) so they cook uniformly.

---

* If the crust looks like it is golden brown and the vegetables are not quite done, line thin strips of aluminum foil around the crust to protect it while you cook the vegetables 5 or so more minutes.

Zucchini Gratinato

Gratinato is the Italian word for au gratin. Au gratin originated from the French and literally means "by grating." Au gratin recipes have sprinkled grated cheese or breadcrumbs (and sometimes both).

INGREDIENTS

3 cups zucchini, thinly sliced (See Removing Moisture from Zucchini in Tips)

1 cup mozzarella, grated

½ cup parmesan, finely grated

1 cup ricotta (optional)

SAUCE*

1 tablespoon olive oil

1 cup unseasoned crushed tomatoes

3 tablespoons tomato paste

½ teaspoon Italian seasoning

½ teaspoon granulated garlic

½ teaspoon coarse salt

⅛ teaspoon ground black pepper

¾ ounce fresh basil or 1 large sprig

INSTRUCTIONS

Prep: Preheat oven to 400°F. Spray 8 x 8" baking dish with cooking oil.

1. Mix sauce ingredients together (if not using purchased sauce).
2. Layer ingredients (similar to lasagna), starting with sauce, zucchini pieces next, cheeses, and top with more sauce and sprinkle with basil. Repeat until all zucchini is used, ending with sauce on top.
3. Cook for 15 minutes covered, then uncover, and lower temperature to 350°F. Continue cooking for 45 minutes.

Top with additional mozzarella if desired.

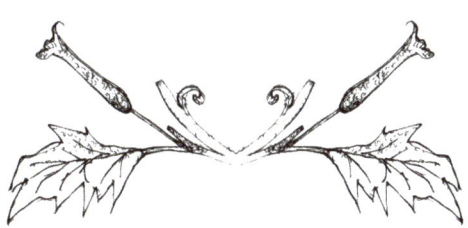

---

* Option: substitute purchased pasta sauce and eliminate sauce ingredients.

Easy Cheesy Zucchini Rice

This rice has the creamy texture of risotto without a lot of stirring. You don't have to squeeze the liquid out of the zucchini because this rice absorbs it and it adds to the creaminess of the dish.

INGREDIENTS

- 1 cup onion, diced
- 1–2 cloves of garlic, minced
- 1 cup long grain rice
- 2 cups chicken stock or vegetable broth
- 1½ cups zucchini, shredded
- 1 cup cheddar cheese, shredded
- ⅓ cup parmesan cheese, grated
- ½ teaspoon salt
- 2 tablespoons butter
- 1 tablespoon olive oil
- Pepper to taste

INSTRUCTIONS

1. Sauté onions in 1 tablespoon butter and 1 tablespoon olive oil.
2. Add garlic and rice after onions are translucent. Cook together until rice is lightly toasted.
3. Pour chicken stock and zucchini into pan, bring to a boil, cover and turn down heat to simmer. Cook for 20–30 minutes – until liquid is gone.
4. Stir in cheeses and remaining butter. Stir to combine. Season to taste.

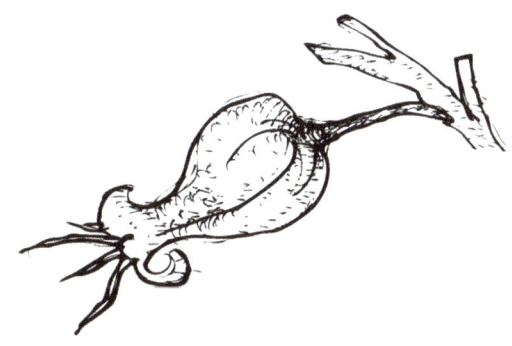

SIDE DISHES

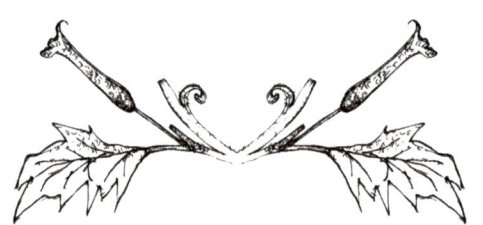

Old-Fashioned Zucchini Bread

My mother created a lot of zucchini recipes back in the '60s and this was one of her best. She used four different spices (cinnamon, cloves, nutmeg, and allspice), which I think is one of the keys to the tasty flavor of this bread.

She'd make many loaves of bread trying to perfect her recipe and by late in the summer season would be baking loaves for freezing and giving away as gifts, or bringing to a "coffee klatch" as women did back in the day. She was very proud of her zucchini creations and if she were alive today (after being encouraged by yours truly), she would have probably published her own book of zucchini recipes.

Recipe makes 1 large loaf or 2 medium sized loaves.

INGREDIENTS

- 3 eggs
- ½ cup canola oil
- 1½ cups sugar (I cut the sugar in half for this recipe using only ¾ cup sugar because I don't like it sweet)
- 2 cups zucchini, grated
- 2 teaspoons vanilla

In a separate bowl:
- 3 cups flour
- 1 teaspoon baking soda
- ¼ teaspoon baking powder
- ½ teaspoon salt
- 1 teaspoon cloves
- 1 teaspoon nutmeg
- 1 teaspoon allspice
- 3 teaspoons cinnamon
- Option: ½ cup crushed nuts (I used walnuts)

INSTRUCTIONS

Prep: Preheat oven to 350°F. Spray bread pan(s) with cooking oil.

1. Beat eggs lightly, then add the next 4 ingredients (oil, sugar, zucchini and vanilla).
2. Combine all dry ingredients in a separate bowl.
3. Add dry ingredients (flour mixture) to egg mixture and blend well.
4. Add nuts if using.
5. Bake for 1 hour.

☞ **Note:** I crush the nuts by putting them in a zipped sandwich bag and hitting the bag with the end of a rolling pin. This method breaks them up quickly and keeps the mess inside a bag.

Carrot Apple Zucchini Bread

This bread is like a carrot cake, zucchini bread and apple muffin all tied into one. I love the combination of flavors with these ingredients. It's a party in your mouth! Definitely, a must try!

Recipe makes 2 medium-sized loaves.

INGREDIENTS

- 1 cup butter, melted
- 1½ cups sugar
- 3 eggs, room temperature
- ¼ cup fresh orange juice
- 1 tablespoon vanilla extract
- 3¼ cups all-purpose flour
- ½ teaspoon salt
- 2½ teaspoons baking powder
- ¾ teaspoon baking soda
- 1 tablespoon cinnamon
- ⅛ teaspoon ground cloves
- ⅛ teaspoon ground nutmeg
- 2 cups zucchini, unpeeled and shredded
- 1 cup carrots, shredded
- 1 cup apple, peeled and shredded

INSTRUCTIONS

Prep: Preheat oven to 350°F. Prepare two 8 x 4" loaf pans (line with parchment and spray with cooking spray).

1. Wet ingredients: blend butter and sugar together, add in eggs, orange juice and vanilla.
2. Dry ingredients: whisk together flour, salt, baking powder, baking soda, cinnamon, cloves and nutmeg.
3. Fold dry ingredients into wet ingredients along with carrots, zucchini and apples.
4. Pour into prepared pans.
5. Bake until golden brown, approximately 1 hour, or until loaves spring back when gently pressed with fingers.

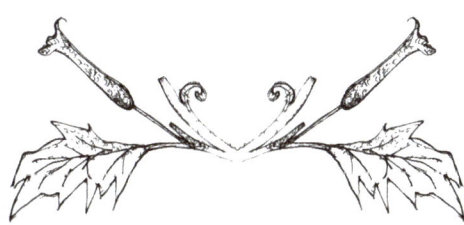

BREADS, MUFFINS & MORE

Zucchini Lemon Bread

Zucchini and lemon go well together, so it's natural that they should be paired in bread. This recipe is almost cake-like. I used Bob's Red Mill® Cake Flour, so that may be why it tasted so light. I toyed with the idea of using Limoncello in place of lemon juice in this recipe but thought I should try it "sober" first and can play with alcoholic ingredients the next time I make it.

The lemon tanginess may have converted me to naming this zucchini bread one of the favorites that I have tried over the years.

INGREDIENTS

- 1 cup sugar
- 6 tablespoons olive oil
- 2 eggs, room temperature
- ⅓ cup milk
- 2 tablespoons lemon juice
- 1 teaspoon vanilla extract
- 2 cups cake flour (I used Bob's Red Mill® brand)
- 1¼ teaspoons baking powder
- ½ teaspoon salt
- 1½ cups zucchini, shredded, drained, and squeezed dry
- 2 tablespoons lemon zest

INSTRUCTIONS

Prep: Preheat oven to 350°F. Prepare a bread pan with baking spray and line with parchment paper. Set aside.

1. In a large mixing bowl, add the sugar and olive oil. Whisk to combine.
2. Add eggs and milk and whisk together.
3. Stir in lemon juice and vanilla extract.
4. In a medium bowl, whisk together flour, baking powder, and salt.
5. Add flour mixture to wet mixture and stir until incorporated.
6. Fold in zucchini and lemon zest.
7. Pour batter into the prepared pan and bake for 45 to 55 minutes.
8. Test for doneness by inserting a toothpick into the batter. It should come out cleanish. The top of the bread should look dry.
9. Cool for about 15 minutes.
10. Use the parchment paper to carefully lift the bread from the pan. Let cool completely on rack.

☞ **Note:** You can frost this bread with a glaze of powdered sugar and lemon juice if you wish.

Blueberry Yogurt Zucchini Bread

Blueberries don't have to be in season to enjoy this bread. I used blueberries I had in the freezer harvested from our berry bushes earlier in the year. And using blueberry yogurt adds even more blueberry flavor.

Because this bread is so moist, baking times will vary based on the moisture content of zucchini, blueberries, climate, and oven variances. Watch the bread, not the clock, and don't worry if it takes more or less time to bake than the baking time listed.

INGREDIENTS

- 1 large egg
- ½ cup light brown sugar, packed
- ⅓ cup canola or vegetable oil (or eliminate oil and use yogurt only)
- ¼ cup granulated sugar
- ¼ cup low-fat Greek yogurt, blueberry flavored or plain (or ½ cup if eliminating oil)
- 1 teaspoon vanilla extract
- 1 cup all-purpose flour plus ¼ cup for tossing with blueberries
- ½ teaspoon baking powder
- ½ teaspoon baking soda
- ¼ teaspoon salt
- 1 cup coarsely grated zucchini, laid loosely in cup and not packed (don't wring out)
- 1 cup (6 ounces) blueberries, fresh or frozen

INSTRUCTIONS

Prep: Preheat oven to 350°F. Spray a 9 x 5" loaf pan with cooking spray or oil and flour the pan; set aside.

1. Combine the first 6 ingredients, through vanilla, in a large bowl and whisk together.
2. Add 1 cup flour, baking powder, baking soda and salt, and stir until just mixed together; don't overmix.
3. Add the zucchini and stir to combine.
4. In another bowl, coat the blueberries with ¼ cup flour.
5. Add the blueberries to the bowl with wet and dry ingredients and fold ingredients together lightly.
6. Pour batter out into the prepared pan, smoothing the top lightly with a spatula. Option: sprinkle the top of the bread with a handful of blueberries for a pop of color.
7. Bake for about 1 hour, until the top is golden, the center is set, and a toothpick inserted in the center comes out clean, or with a few moist crumbs, but no batter.
8. Allow bread to cool in the pan for about 15 minutes before turning out on a wire rack to cool completely before slicing.

Snickerdoodle Swirl Bread

Snickerdoodle cookies are a favorite among many children and adults. Why not enjoy those flavors merged into zucchini bread? This bread just melts in your mouth with the combination of the cinnamon/sugar flavors. It doubles as a sweet treat for breakfast or dessert.

INGREDIENTS

- 3 cups all-purpose flour
- 2 teaspoons cinnamon
- ½ teaspoon allspice
- 1 teaspoon baking soda
- ½ teaspoon baking powder
- 1 teaspoon salt

- 1 cup oil
- 3 eggs
- 1¾ cups granulated sugar
- 1 teaspoon vanilla extract
- 2 cups grated zucchini (about 1 large zucchini), squeezed dry in clean tea towel

CINNAMON SWIRL

- ½ cup granulated sugar
- 1 teaspoon cinnamon

INSTRUCTIONS

Prep: Preheat oven to 350°F. Grease and flour two standard sized loaf pans and set aside.

1. In a large bowl, combine flour, cinnamon, allspice, baking soda, baking powder and salt. Whisk together.
2. In a separate bowl, beat oil, eggs, sugar and vanilla until well mixed.
3. Pour the egg mixture into the flour mixture and stir together until fully combined. Batter will be thick.
4. Add zucchini and mix until distributed throughout batter.
5. In a small bowl, combine cinnamon swirl ingredients and set aside.
6. Pour half the batter into prepared pans and sprinkle with ¾ of the cinnamon sugar mixture.
7. Cover with remaining batter and sprinkle with the rest of the cinnamon sugar on top of the bread batter.
8. Bake for 50–60 minutes or until a knife is inserted and comes out clean. Rest in pan for 5 minutes and turn out bread onto wire rack. Allow to cool before slicing.

Cinnamon Roll Zucchini Bread

Cinnamon roll zucchini bread – I'll bet you can't believe it would taste even remotely similar to real cinnamon rolls. Well it does, I guarantee you! I gave this bread to a friend who doesn't like vegetables; in fact he runs away from anything green in food and is very suspicious if you try to hide vegetables in any dish you share with him. He loved it! I didn't even have to hide the fact that the bread was made with zucchini.

INGREDIENTS

1¾ cups all-purpose flour	¾ cup granulated sugar
1 teaspoon baking powder	2 teaspoon vanilla
¼ teaspoon baking soda	2 eggs
¼ teaspoon salt	¾ cup non-fat plain Greek yogurt
¼ cup butter at room temperature	1 cup shredded zucchini (peeled or unpeeled)

CINNAMON SWIRL LAYER

2½ tablespoons white sugar	2 teaspoons cinnamon
2½ tablespoons brown sugar	1 tablespoon water (option – see note below)

VANILLA ICING

½ cup powdered sugar	1–2 teaspoons milk
1 teaspoon vanilla	

INSTRUCTIONS

Prep: Preheat oven to 350°F. Line a 9 x 5" bread pan with parchment paper, leaving a slight overhang, and spray with cooking spray; set aside.

1. Combine the flour, baking powder, baking soda and salt in a medium sized bowl.
2. In a large bowl, beat the butter, sugar and vanilla using an electric mixer until creamy.
3. Add the eggs, one at a time, beating well after each addition.
4. Add the yogurt and mix well.
5. Stir in the shredded zucchini.
6. Add dry ingredients to wet and stir together until just combined.
7. Spread half of the batter into the prepared bread pan.
8. Stir together all of the cinnamon swirl layer ingredients and spread over batter, leaving a small border around the edge. Top with remaining bread batter and spread out evenly.
9. Bake in preheated oven for 50 minutes or until a toothpick inserted in the center comes out clean. (As the bread bakes, it will create swirls of cinnamon sugar throughout.)
10. Remove from oven and cool in pan 10 minutes, then remove from pan and cool completely on wire rack before topping with vanilla icing.

VANILLA ICING

Combine powdered sugar, vanilla, and 1 teaspoon of milk. Stir together until smooth. If it's too thick, add a tiny bit more milk. Pour over cooled bread.

☞ **Note:** I tried two ways of doing the cinnamon swirl. I added water to the mixture one time and next batch I left it dry. I preferred it dry, easier to spread over the batter.

Chocolate Zucchini Muffins

Chocolate makes everything taste good — that is, if you are a chocolate lover like me. If you are a chocolate purist, combining cocoa and chocolate chips is about as chocolate as you can get. And even if you think chocolate is just so-so, these muffins may change your mind.

In an effort to make these muffins a little healthier (even though we all know chocolate is good for you), I eliminated oil and sugar, substituting in Greek yogurt and a baking sugar substitute.

Makes 1 dozen regular sized muffins.

INGREDIENTS

- 1½ cups zucchini, shredded
- 2 large eggs
- ½ cup nonfat plain Greek yogurt
- ¼ cup Truvía® natural sweetener (or substitute ½ cup granulated white sugar, if you prefer)
- 1 teaspoon vanilla extract
- 1 cup all-purpose flour
- ½ cup unsweetened cocoa powder
- ¾ teaspoon baking soda
- ¼ teaspoon baking powder
- ¼ teaspoon salt
- ¾ cup semi-sweet chocolate chips

INSTRUCTIONS

Prep: Preheat the oven to 375°F. Spray muffin tin with cooking spray and set aside.

1. Shred the zucchini. Lightly squeeze the zucchini in cheesecloth or towel to pull out some of the moisture, leaving it a little moist.
2. In a large mixing bowl, whisk together eggs, yogurt, sugar, vanilla and zucchini until smooth.
3. Add flour, cocoa, baking soda, baking powder, and salt to the wet ingredients, mixing well to combine. I use a whisk to fully incorporate everything.
4. Drop in the chocolate chips and stir well.
5. Scoop the batter into the prepared muffin tin, filling each cup ¾ full.
6. Bake for 20–25 minutes. When you lightly press the top, it should spring back. Remove from oven and let cool, in the pan, on a wire rack. When it is cool enough to handle the pan, tip muffins out.

Store in an airtight bag in the refrigerator or wrap cooled muffins in plastic wrap and freeze in an airtight bag.

Cheesy Zucchini Biscuits

Are you a fan of cheese biscuits? Then you'll want to try these cheesy zucchini biscuits. They are not your typical light and fluffy biscuits. They are a dense full-bodied delightful cheese-flavored biscuit that pairs well with meals.

Yields approximately 10 biscuits.

INGREDIENTS

- 1 cup shredded zucchini
- 2½ cups all-purpose flour
- ¾ teaspoon salt, separated ¼ and ½ teaspoon
- 1 tablespoon baking powder
- ½ cup cold butter, cubed
- ½ cup shredded cheddar cheese
- ¼ cup shredded part skim mozzarella cheese
- ¼ cup shredded parmesan cheese
- 2 tablespoons chopped oil-packed sun-dried tomatoes (or use fresh tomatoes mixed with a dash of olive oil)
- 2 teaspoons dried basil
- 1 cup milk plus a few tablespoons (as needed)

INSTRUCTIONS

Prep: Preheat oven to 425°F.

1. Place the shredded zucchini in a colander, sprinkle with ¼ teaspoon salt and mix. Let zucchini drain for about 10 minutes.
2. Rinse and drain zucchini well. Squeeze zucchini in a towel to remove the excess liquid.
3. Whisk together the flour, the remaining salt and baking powder. Cut in the butter until the mixture resembles coarse crumbs.
4. Stir in zucchini, cheeses, tomatoes and basil.
5. Add the milk and stir until moistened. Don't overwork dough.
6. Drop by ⅓-cupfuls into a greased 9 x 13" baking dish. Bake for 25 minutes or until golden brown.

Serve warm or at room temperature.

Cornbread Muffins

What I like about these corn muffins is:

- They complement many different meals, soups, stews, chilis, and even salads, roasts and ribs.
- They freeze well for the future.
- They are a good individual size, no messy cutting to size; you can even make them into "minis."
- And they taste great!

Makes 12–18 muffins (depending on muffin tin size) or 24–36 mini muffins.

INGREDIENTS

- 3 cups zucchini, shredded
- 1 cup cornmeal
- 1 cup all-purpose flour (or substitute cake flour for lighter muffins)
- ¼ cup sugar
- 1½ teaspoons baking powder
- ½ teaspoon baking soda
- 1 teaspoon salt
- 1 cup milk (or substitute low-fat buttermilk)
- ¼ cup butter (room temperature)
- 2 eggs
- 1 cup corn, fresh or frozen (about 2 corn cobs)

INSTRUCTIONS

Prep: Preheat oven to 400°F. Spray muffin tin with cooking oil.

1. Squeeze shredded zucchini in a tea towel, releasing liquid. Zucchini should be dryish. Set aside.
2. Combine dry ingredients: cornmeal, flour, sugar, baking powder, baking soda and salt.
3. Whisk wet ingredients together: milk, butter and eggs.
4. Mix wet into dry ingredients, folding into a batter. Add zucchini and corn to batter.
5. Pour batter into muffin tin, filling each cup close to the top. Bake for 25–30 minutes.

Cool on wire rack for 10 minutes.

Light and Savory Courgette Scones

For all my friends in the British Isles, this recipe is for you! A light and savory scone that is delightful served with tea any time of day. These scones will also nicely complement an evening meal.

Makes 12 scones.

INGREDIENTS

- 12.5 ounces (2½ cups) all-purpose flour
- 2½ teaspoons baking powder
- ¾ teaspoon salt
- ¾ teaspoon black pepper
- 4 ounces (8 tablespoons) butter, cold and cut into pieces
- 3 ounces (⅓ cup) heavy cream (option: substitute ⅓ cup ricotta cheese)
- 1 egg
- 8 ounces (1 cup) courgette (zucchini), grated and squeezed dry in a clean tea towel
- 8 ounces (1 cup) sharp cheddar, grated plus extra for topping scones

INSTRUCTIONS

Prep: Preheat oven to 200°C (400°F). Line a baking sheet with parchment paper.

1. Fit a food processor with a dough blade, and pulse together flour, baking powder, salt and pepper.
2. Add butter and process until little crumbs start to form.
3. Pour in heavy cream (or ricotta cheese if using), egg, courgette and cheddar to the mixture in the food processor. Process until everything has combined. A soft dough will form.
4. Turn out dough onto a lightly floured surface and press into a large 1" thick circle. Transfer the dough to the prepared baking sheet.
5. Cut 12 equal sized wedges with a sharp knife and spread them apart so they have room to grow during baking.
6. Bake in the oven for about 20 minutes. Sprinkle with extra cheddar cheese if desired. Serve warm.

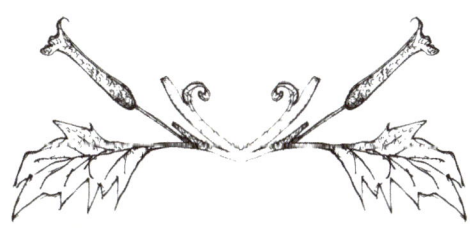

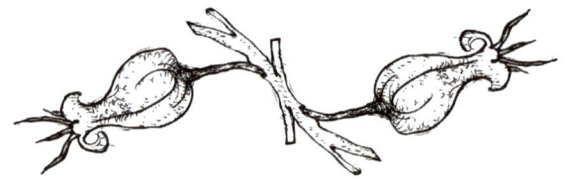

Oat Nut Chocolate Chip Cookies

Anyone who knows me understands that cookies are my kryptonite so I don't make them as often as I'd like. But sometimes I just have to make a batch, and zucchini surplus is as good an excuse as any to do so.

I improvised with the ingredients, using my mother's 1960s zucchini bread recipe as a base. I added oats to make it a little healthier and chocolate chips because…well, it's chocolate! Oh, I guess that negates the healthy part, but chocolate enthusiasts might argue that point. They came out great, but I'm probably not a good judge, since I think about any cookie is good.

And if you want, you can spread a glaze on them. My recommendation is Limoncello Glaze.

INGREDIENTS

1½ cups all-purpose flour*

1 cup oats

1½ cup zucchini, grated

1½ heaping teaspoons ground cinnamon

¼ teaspoon cloves

¼ teaspoon allspice

⅛ teaspoon nutmeg

½ teaspoon baking soda

½ cup (1 stick) butter, softened

½–¾ cup granulated sugar (depending on how sweet you like your cookies)

1 large egg

1 teaspoon vanilla extract

OPTIONAL INGREDIENTS

1 cup chopped nuts

1 cup chocolate chips (regular or minis, milk or dark chocolate)

---

* Flour options: whole wheat or oat flour will make cookies a little denser in texture. You can also use half all-purpose flour and half whole wheat or oat flour.

INSTRUCTIONS

Prep: Preheat oven to 350°F. Prepare baking sheets with parchment paper or Silpat® sheet.

1. Combine flour, oats, cinnamon, nutmeg, cloves, allspice and baking soda in a small bowl.
2. In a large bowl mix butter and sugar with a mixer until smooth.
3. Add egg and vanilla extract to butter/sugar mixture.
4. Add zucchini.
5. Gradually beat in dry ingredients (flour mixture).
6. Stir in nuts and chocolate chips (if using).
7. Drop by rounded teaspoonful 2" apart onto prepared baking sheets.
8. Bake for 10–12 minutes or until light golden brown.
9. Cool on wire rack or on paper towels.
10. Glaze if desired (see below).

☞ **Note:** I added both nuts and chocolate chips to my cookies.

Limoncello Glaze

INGREDIENTS

½ cup powdered sugar

2–3 tablespoons Limoncello (see Tips for Limoncello Liqueur recipe resource) or substitute lemon juice

INSTRUCTIONS

1. Whisk ingredients together to reach a spreadable consistency. For a thicker glaze add more powdered sugar.
2. Spoon over cooled cookies or warm cookies if you want a thin glaze coverage.
3. If glaze is thick, spread it over the cookie with a knife.

Chocolate Zookies

My husband likes about anything with chocolate in it. In fact, I put a dash of chocolate in chili, which he swears makes it taste better. When I came up with these chocolate zookies he was so very happy, he volunteered to clean up the kitchen. I don't know if you'll have the same outcome in your house, but if the only results are these delicious chocolate zookies, that's okay!

INGREDIENTS

- 1⅓ cups all-purpose flour
- ½ cup unsweetened cocoa powder
- ½ teaspoon baking soda
- ¼ teaspoon baking powder
- ¼ teaspoon salt
- 2 large eggs
- ½ cup plain Greek yogurt (nonfat or whole)
- ½ cup granulated sugar (or ¼ cup sugar blend substitute)
- 1 teaspoon vanilla extract
- 1¼ cups shredded zucchini (squeezed dry in a clean tea towel)
- ¾ cup semi-sweet chocolate chips

OPTIONAL ICING

- ½ cup powdered sugar
- 2 tablespoons milk

INSTRUCTIONS

Prep: Preheat oven to 375°F and line cookie sheets with parchment paper, or Silpat® sheet.

1. Combine dry ingredients together: flour, cocoa powder, baking soda, baking powder and salt.
2. Mix together separately: eggs, yogurt, sugar, vanilla and zucchini.
3. Stir wet and dry ingredients together.
4. Drop in the chocolate chips and stir well.
5. Place teaspoon-sized cookie dough balls onto prepared cookie sheets and bake for 10–12 minutes.

OPTIONAL ICING

Frost cookies with a powdered sugar icing if you want to add a little sweetness. Whisk the powdered sugar with the milk, adding the milk a little at a time until desired thickness. Frost by spreading thicker icing with a knife or drizzling over cookies if thinner mixture.

DESSERTS

Lemon Ricotta Cookies

Lemon ricotta cookies are a special Italian cookie typically made from a recipe handed down generation-to-generation. I make homemade ricotta so these cookies have an extra boost of love in them; however, a store brand ricotta works in this recipe too. The ricotta cheese and zucchini pack this cookie with moisture and pillow softness.

INGREDIENTS

- ¾ cup butter
- ½ cup sugar
- 1 egg
- Zest of 1 lemon
- 3 tablespoons ricotta (store brand or homemade; see Tips for resource to recipe)
- 1 cup zucchini, unpeeled and shredded (squeezed dry in clean tea towel)
- 2 cups all-purpose flour
- 1 teaspoon baking powder
- ½ teaspoon salt

OPTIONAL ICING

- ½–¾ cup powdered sugar
- 1–2 tablespoons lemon juice

INSTRUCTIONS

Prep: Preheat oven to 375°F. Line baking sheets with non-stick foil.

1. Cream butter and sugar together.
2. Mix egg, lemon zest and ricotta until fluffy. Add to butter and sugar mixture.
3. Combine zucchini into wet ingredients.
4. Whisk together flour, baking powder, and salt. Add to wet ingredients and mix well.
5. Drop dough by teaspoonfuls onto baking sheets. Bake for 15–20 minutes or until lightly browned.

OPTIONAL ICING

Mix powdered sugar with lemon juice or kick it up a notch and replace lemon juice with Limoncello (see Tips for Limoncello Liqueur recipe resource). Drizzle icing over cookies after they come out of the oven and while warm.

Traditional Ziggy Figgy Bars

These ziggy figgy bars can be prepared two ways. One version uses more traditional flour ingredients and the other is for people who need a gluten-free recipe (next page). Try them both!

INGREDIENTS

FILLING

- 2 cups chopped/cubed zucchini, unpeeled (will cook down to ½ cup)
- ¼ cup water
- ¼ cup fig jam
- 2 tablespoons orange juice
- 2 teaspoons honey
- 1 teaspoon quick cooking tapioca (or substitute cornstarch)
- ⅛ teaspoon cinnamon

DOUGH

- 1 cup all-purpose flour
- ¾ cup white whole wheat flour (I used Bob's Red Mill®)
- ½ teaspoon baking powder
- Pinch of salt
- 1 egg
- 1 teaspoon pure vanilla extract
- 1 teaspoon orange zest
- ½ cup butter, softened
- ¼ cup brown sugar (packed)

INSTRUCTIONS

Prep: Preheat oven to 350°F. Line a baking sheet with parchment paper or Silpat® sheet.

1. Cook zucchini in water until translucent. Drain well and mash.
2. Add the remaining filling ingredients to pan and continue to cook for another 5–7 minutes or until thickened. Cool filling.
3. Follow instructions for making the dough and assembling cookies from gluten-free recipe on the next page.

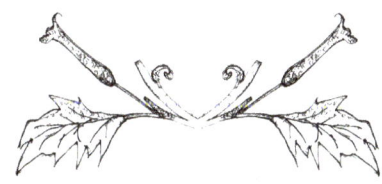

DESSERTS

Gluten-Free Ziggy Figgy Bars

INGREDIENTS

FILLING

- 1 cup zucchini (skin on), shredded and squeezed dry
- 2 tablespoons fig jam
- 1 tablespoon orange zest
- 1 tablespoon orange juice, fresh squeezed if possible
- 2 tablespoons pure maple syrup
- 1 teaspoon quick cooking tapioca, cornstarch or substitute
- Sprinkle each of cinnamon, cloves and nutmeg (heavier on the cinnamon)
- Pinch of salt

DOUGH

- 1 cup almond flour
- ¼ cup coconut flour
- ¼ cup tapioca flour (or substitute cornstarch, arrowroot starch or quick cooking tapioca. I used quick cooking tapioca)
- Pinch of salt
- 1 egg
- 2 tablespoons maple syrup
- ¼ cup butter, cubed

INSTRUCTIONS

Prep: Preheat oven to 350°F. Line a baking sheet with parchment paper or Silpat® sheet.

Prepare filling: In a saucepan combine all the filling ingredients. Cook over medium heat until mixture turns into a thick paste. Remove and cool while preparing dough.

Prepare dough: Whisk flours and salt together to combine. Stir in egg and maple syrup. Add softened butter into flour/egg mixture. Refrigerate dough for 15–20 minutes.

ASSEMBLE COOKIES

1. Lay out a sheet of plastic wrap on the counter. Place cookie dough on top. Layer another sheet of plastic wrap on top of the dough. Roll out to about ¼" thick. (Think of how thick a store bought Fig Newton® crust is and gauge your dough.) Dough should be about 5–6" wide and about 12–14" long. (Recipe makes about two logs of dough.)
2. Spread filling about 1½" wide all down the center of the dough. Carefully wrap one side of the dough over, and then the other side so all the filling is covered. (Use the bottom sheet of plastic wrap to help you fold over the dough if needed.)
3. Place cookie logs on prepared baking sheet and cook for about 20–25 minutes or until they are slightly golden around the edges.
4. Let cookies cool about 10 minutes and then cut into 2" slices and set on a wire rack to cool completely.

DESSERTS

Brownies

These are award-winning brownies in more than one way. My classic T-bird won an award at a car show and I wanted to thank the team at the local detail shop for putting the perfect shine on my car so I baked these brownies. I was careful to explain that the green bits in these brownies were zucchini, honestly, just zucchini!

INGREDIENTS

- ½ cup canola oil or olive oil
- 1½ cups sugar or ¾ cup sugar blend (I used Truvía® natural sweetener)
- 2 teaspoons vanilla extract
- 2 cups whole-wheat pastry flour or all-purpose unbleached flour
- ½ cup unsweetened cocoa powder
- 1½ teaspoons baking soda
- 1 teaspoon salt
- 2 cups zucchini, shredded (squeezed dryish)
- Option: Add ½ cup chopped nuts and/or chocolate chips.

INSTRUCTIONS

Prep: Preheat oven to 350°F. Grease and flour an 8 x 11" baking dish.

1. Thoroughly combine oil, sugar and vanilla extract in a bowl.
2. Whisk together flour, cocoa, baking soda and salt in a separate bowl.
3. Combine wet ingredients and dry ingredients. The batter will be crumbly.
4. Stir zucchini into batter. Batter should be moist and thick.
5. Option: stir in nuts and/or chocolate chips.
6. Pour the batter into the prepared baking dish.
7. Bake for approximately 25–30 minutes or until brownies are fairly firm and begin to pull from the sides of the pan.
8. Slice into 12 brownies after cooled.

☞ **Note:** If you like your brownies frosted, add a layer of chocolate chips on top of brownie mixture before baking and smooth melted chips on brownies when finished baking and while still hot.

Limoncello Cake

This is a really easy cake recipe because it cheats a bit on ingredient prep. By using a store-bought cake mix and pudding mix, the dry ingredients are assembled for you. All you have to do is measure and add the wet ingredients and bake.

Limoncello cake gets rave reviews every time I serve it. Check Tips for recipe resource to Limoncello Liqueur. And if Limoncello is not a favorite liqueur of yours, substitute lemon juice wherever Limoncello is listed in the recipe. It's good either way.

INGREDIENTS

- 1 package lemon cake mix
- 1 package lemon instant pudding
- 3 eggs
- 1½ cups zucchini, shredded
- ½ cup water
- ½ cup canola oil
- ½ cup Limoncello (see Tips for Limoncello recipe resource)

INSTRUCTIONS

Prep: Preheat oven to 350°F. Coat bundt pan with non-stick spray.

1. Mix together all ingredients (hand-mix in bowl or beat with electric mixer) and put into prepared bundt pan.
2. Bake for 40–50 minutes.
3. Cool, loosen slightly from sides, invert onto cooling rack or serving platter.

☞ **Note:** This cake can be made in bundt pan, bread pans for pound cake, or cupcake/muffin tins.

FROSTING OR TOPPING OPTIONS

Sprinkle with powdered sugar or make a glaze of 2 cups powdered sugar and ¼ cup Limoncello. Poke a few holes into cake and drizzle glaze over it. Or just drizzle glaze without poking holes, your choice.

Cheesecake Cupcakes

Family members and friends will devour these cheesecake cupcakes hot out of the oven or cooled and drizzled with chocolate sauce. After I made a batch of them, I delivered a few to a neighbor couple who ate them on the spot as we were chatting. Their approval was a big thumbs-up.

I used my homemade ricotta for the cheese filling (see Tips for the recipe resources). Cream cheese could be substituted instead of ricotta. Also, a quick confession, the first time I made these cupcakes I forgot the egg that goes into the cupcake batter. Oops – and they still turned out great.

INGREDIENTS

CUPCAKE BATTER

- 1½ cups all-purpose flour (option: cake flour for lighter cupcake)
- 1 teaspoon baking soda
- ½ teaspoon salt
- ½ cup granulated sugar (or ¼ cup baking blend sugar such as Truvía® natural sweetener)
- ¼ cup oil, vegetable or canola
- 1 egg
- 1 teaspoon vanilla extract
- ½ cup plus 2 tablespoons milk
- 1 cup zucchini, peeled and grated (squeezed firmly to reduce to ½ cup)

CHEESECAKE FILLING

- 8 ounces fresh homemade ricotta (see recipe resource in Tips) or store brand, or substitute cream cheese
- ¼ cup granulated sugar
- 1 egg
- Pinch of salt

INSTRUCTIONS

Prep: Preheat oven to 350°F. Spray a 12-cup muffin tin with cooking oil or line with cupcake papers.

1. Whisk together flour, baking soda and salt.
2. In a separate bowl, blend sugar, oil, egg, vanilla and milk.
3. Mix wet and dry ingredients, and stir in zucchini.
4. Add half the batter into muffin tins.
5. Prepare the cheesecake filling by mixing cheese, sugar, egg, and salt together.
6. Drop a tablespoonful of cheesecake filling into each muffin tin on top of the batter.
7. Cover filling with remaining cupcake batter.
8. Bake for 25–30 minutes. Cupcakes should spring back when lightly touched.

Cool in pan for 5–10 minutes and remove to wire rack to cool further.

Walnut Shortbread Bites

These treats may be small in size, but are large in flavor. When you make them for yourself, you can cut them into larger sizes if that's your preference. I won't tell.

The combination of the brown sugar and walnuts balance the flavors nicely with the zucchini. I served these to a tough crowd (usually non-dessert eaters), and after the dish was passed around and returned to me the plate was empty. Was I surprised!

INGREDIENTS

SHORTBREAD

- 1 cup butter (room temperature)
- ⅔ cup brown sugar, firmly packed
- ½ teaspoon salt
- ¼ teaspoon each of cinnamon, ginger and nutmeg
- 1 teaspoon vanilla
- 2 cups all-purpose flour
- ½ cup walnuts, chopped

FILLING

- ¾ cup zucchini, shredded (moisture tightly squeezed out)
- 1 teaspoon lemon juice
- 1 tablespoon sugar
- ¼ teaspoon each cinnamon and nutmeg

INSTRUCTIONS

Prep: Preheat oven to 350°F. Spray 9 x 9" baking dish with cooking spray.

1. Mix wet ingredients: cream butter and sugar, then add salt, spices and vanilla.
2. Combine flour into butter/sugar mixture slowly, about ½ cup at a time.
3. Pat about ⅔ of the dough into the baking dish as even as possible. Flour hands if needed.
4. For filling, mix zucchini with lemon juice, sugar and spices.
5. Spread zucchini filling over shortbread crust.
6. Stir walnuts into the remaining dough and crumble over the top of the zucchini.
7. Bake for 35 minutes or until lightly browned.

Cool and cut into bite-sized pieces.

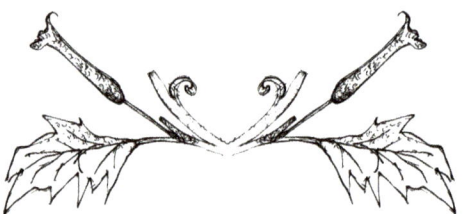

Condiments

Zesto (Zucchini Pesto)

I started making this zesto when I had an unusually small crop of basil in my garden one year. I needed something to add to the basil to make my annual pesto recipe. So I added zucchini – a great pesto substitute! I was amazed at how flavorful this zesto turned out. It has become the "end of summer" zesto I make when the basil is almost gone and I have a few zucchini left to use from the garden.

INGREDIENTS

- 2 cups grated zucchini
- 1–2 cloves garlic, roughly chopped
- 2 tablespoons pine nuts
- ½ cup grated parmesan cheese
- ¼ cup fresh basil leaves
- ½ teaspoon sesame seeds or tahini
- Generous dash of Spice Islands® organic garlic & herb seasoning
- Salt & pepper to taste
- 2–4 tablespoons extra virgin olive oil

INSTRUCTIONS

1. Thoroughly squeeze all excess water from the grated zucchini in a clean tea towel or cheesecloth.
2. Place zucchini in a food processor along with garlic, pine nuts, parmesan, basil, sesame seeds or tahini, seasonings and salt & pepper.
3. With the food processor running, drizzle in the olive oil until the zesto pesto reaches the consistency of pesto.

Let mixture rest for 1–2 minutes. Check for flavor and adjust seasonings as necessary

Sweet Relish

Sweet pickle relish in my house has now been replaced by this sweet zucchini relish. The flavor of the zucchini relish is far superior to the store brand pickle relish and I've heard the same comments from taste testers of this recipe.

The bonus is that the recipe uses 14 cups of zucchini if you make the full recipe and if you don't have a bumper crop of squash, cut the recipe in half or one-quarter.

Yield: 9–10 half-pint canning jars.

INGREDIENTS

- 14 cups zucchini, grated
- 4 cups onions, chopped
- 4 cups red bell peppers, chopped
- 5–6 tablespoons salt
- 6 cups sugar
- 1 tablespoon cornstarch (mixed with a little water to dissolve it)
- ¾ teaspoon ground nutmeg
- 1 teaspoon turmeric
- 2½ cups white vinegar
- 1½ teaspoons celery seed
- ½ teaspoon coarse black pepper

INSTRUCTIONS

1. Grate zucchini in food processor in batches along with onion and bell peppers.
2. Sprinkle salt over vegetables and mix. Cover and let stand in the fridge overnight.
3. Next day, rinse thoroughly in a large strainer and drain well.
4. Place vegetable mixture into a large pan and add the remaining ingredients.
5. Bring to a boil over medium high heat, then reduce the heat to medium low and simmer for 30 minutes.
6. Sterilize 10 8-ounce jars and lids. Pack and seal in hot sterilized jars. Fill jars just shy of the top.
7. Refrigerate when cool or hot water bath if canning. (For complete canning instructions, consult canning guide.)

☞ **Tip:** Don't want relish quite so sweet? Add 1 teaspoon dry mustard.

Strawberry Pineapple Jelly

This jelly is the perfect pairing of ingredients. Strawberry and pineapple make a good blend of flavors, but if you prefer orange and pineapple, or cherry, whatever combinations suit you, try them out with this jelly. And I dare you to taste the zucchini – it fooled many a critical taste tester.

Makes 8–9 half-pint jars.

INGREDIENTS

- 6 cups zucchini, seeded, shredded, peeled
- 6 cups sugar
- ½ cup lemon juice
- 1 can (20 ounces) crushed pineapple
- 1 package (6 ounces) strawberry gelatin
- 1 package (2 ounces) fruit pectin

INSTRUCTIONS

1. In a large pot, bring the zucchini and sugar to a boil over medium-high heat. Stir constantly for 5–6 minutes.
2. Add lemon juice and pineapple. Reduce heat to medium, cook and stir for 8 minutes.
3. Add gelatin and fruit pectin. If mixture is not hot enough to bring to a boil, raise heat to medium-high to boil for about 1 minute. Remove from the heat.
4. Fill jars or plastic containers with jelly mixture. It will be thin until refrigerated and cooled.
5. If storing in the refrigerator or freezer, cool before covering with lids. Refrigerate up to 3 weeks.
6. If preserving, ladle into canning jars while still hot. Use water bath per proper canning instructions.

CONDIMENTS

Pico de Gallo

At the end of summer when the countertops of my kitchen are full of tomatoes AND zucchini, I make several batches of pico de gallo. I've been making this zucchini version of pico de gallo for so long I've forgotten what the traditional pico de gallo ingredients are.

Yields about 4 cups.

INGREDIENTS

- 2 cups zucchini, finely chopped (about 1½ small zucchini)
- 2 cups tomatoes, finely chopped (about 6 Roma tomatoes)
- 1 poblano pepper, seeded and chopped
- ⅓ cup shallot, finely chopped (about 1 medium shallot)
- 1 jalapeño pepper, seeded and diced
- ¼ cup fresh cilantro (loosely packed), finely chopped
- 1 garlic clove, minced
- Juice from ½ lime
- ½ teaspoon salt
- ¼ teaspoon pepper
- Sprinkle of chili powder
- Sprinkle of jalapeño powder (I used Pendery's®)
- Drizzle of olive oil

INSTRUCTIONS

Mix all ingredients together, and refrigerate for a couple of hours before serving. Best prepared a day ahead.

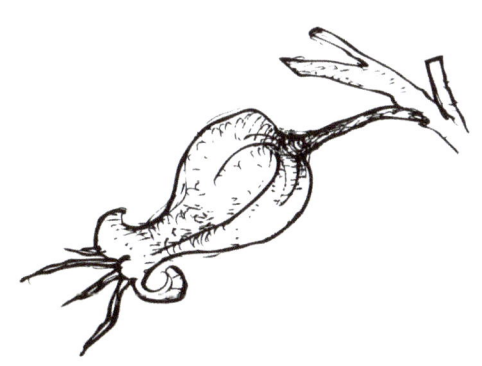

Zucchini Spread

Zucchini caramelized in olive oil, butter and garlic. Oh yeah! Use it on crackers or bread as an appetizer, on sandwiches in place of mayonnaise or mustard, or spread it on bread as a substitute for butter. It's a great spread, no matter how you use it.

INGREDIENTS

5 tablespoons olive oil

2 tablespoons butter

4 cups zucchini, finely shredded

2 teaspoons garlic, minced

Salt and pepper to taste

INSTRUCTIONS

1. Warm olive oil and melt butter in a medium sized skillet.
2. Squeeze liquid out of zucchini in a clean tea towel, and then add to the pan to sauté.
3. Cook over medium low heat, adding garlic after zucchini has cooked down a bit. Keep stirring to prevent charring.
4. Zucchini will caramelize into a soft spreadable jammish consistency.

Store in the refrigerator for up to 1 week.

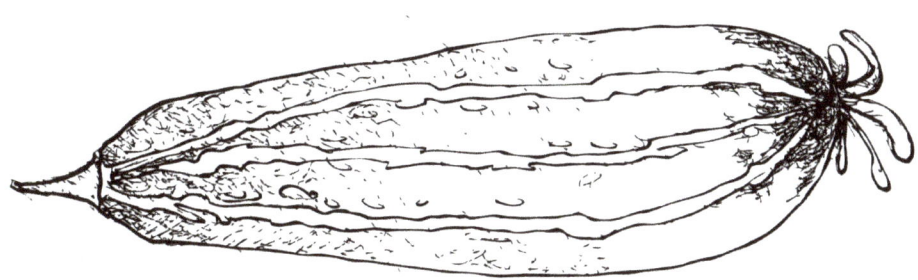

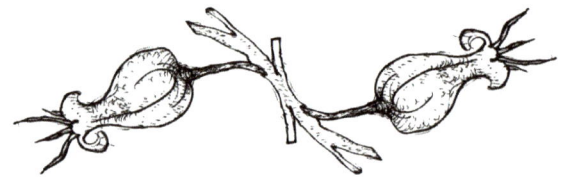

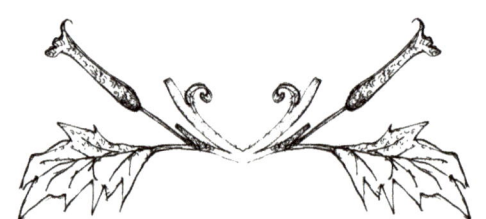

ZUCCHINI, ZUCCHETTA (ITALIAN), TROMBONCINO (ITALIAN), COURGETTES

All of the above names refer to zucchini squash. In the British Isles and Canada, Courgettes is the more common name for zucchini. In Italy, Zucchetta and depending on the type of zucchini squash Tromboncino is used when referring to zucchini. You will note that each of these names have been used in a recipe in this cookbook.

REMOVING MOISTURE FROM ZUCCHINI

There are many opinions on the subject of removing the moisture out of zucchini. I prefer squeezing shredded zucchini in a tea towel or nutmilk bag. And if I am cooking sliced zucchini, depending on the recipe, I might salt and drain it for 10–15 minutes and then pat it dry. I tried the potato ricer method and thought it was too messy and didn't think the results were as good. However, I've included it here for you to decide which method works best for you.

- Lay shredded zucchini in a clean tea towel and squeeze over the sink. Repeat squeezing until liquid stops dripping from the towel.
- Place shredded zucchini in a nutmilk bag and squeeze over the sink. Repeat squeezing until liquid stops dripping.
- Spoon shredded zucchini in a potato ricer and close the ricer mechanism as if you were ricing potatoes. Liquid will escape through the holes in the ricer. Some smaller zucchini bits may also escape.
- Using a colander, layer zucchini slices and salt. Let drain for about 10–15 minutes. Remove from the colander, rinse and pat zucchini dry.

Notice the difference in volume once the zucchini has been squeezed from a tea towel or nutmilk bag. If a recipe asks for 1½ cups shredded zucchini, you may have only 1 cup yield. That's okay.

I may have a few slices of zucchini left over after I have made a recipe. I put these slices in the fridge overnight in a plastic bag with a paper towel to absorb the moisture. The next day the slices are dry and ready to use in another recipe or frozen (removing the paper towel before freezing).

ZUCCHINI GRATING TECHNIQUES

BOX GRATER VERSUS FOOD PROCESSOR

I noticed that when I grated zucchini on the box grater, the zucchini seemed to come out wetter than if I used the food processor. Also, my food processor has two grating sizes, which makes it nice if I want a finer grate on the zucchini. I tend to use the box grater when I'm in a hurry and only need to grate one small zucchini. Setting the box grater on its side with a paper plate underneath is easier for me. The paper plate catches the grated zucchini and is easy to pour by folding the paper plate in half, using it like a funnel. When I have a bigger grating job I pull out the food processor. So at least by my analysis either kitchen tool works grate (play on words – great) and gets the job done.

RECIPE RESOURCES

Homemade Ricotta Cheese https://christinasfoodandtravel.com/did-someone-say-lets-make-ricotta-cheese-im-in/

Limoncello Liqueur https://christinasfoodandtravel.com/when-you-have-lemons-make-limoncello/

Nonna's Crockpot Pasta Sauce https://christinasfoodandtravel.com/nonnas-pasta-sauce-updated-for-todays-busy-lifestyle/

Homemade Vegetable Bouillon https://christinasfoodandtravel.com/soup-er-mix-vegetable-bouillion/

SCARLET RUNNER BEANS

A note about scarlet runner beans: They are a hardy bean that is easy to grow in a backyard garden. They can be found in the dry bean section at farmer's markets and online. You can substitute cranberry beans or borlotti beans for scarlet runner beans.

FLAXSEED

Check https://draxe.com/10-flax-seed-benefits-nutrition-facts/ for more information on the benefits of including flaxseed in your diet. Flaxseed meal can be found at your local grocery store in the baking supplies aisle, at Whole Foods and other "natural foods" markets, or ordered through Amazon or Bob's Red Mill®.

CHIFFONADE

Chiffonade is a cutting technique. It refers to shredding raw leafy lettuces, or any leafy herbs that can be stacked together, rolled into a cylinder shape, and then sliced thinly at a 90-degree angle from the length of the rolled leaves.

Conversion Charts

The recipes in this book are written primarily in American standard measurements and Fahrenheit oven temperatures. Charts are provided to help you convert to measurements and temperatures to fit your cooking needs.

You could also use an instant US/Metric/UK conversion calculator from Convert-Me.com.

The charts below use standard U.S. measures following U.S. Government guidelines. The charts offer equivalents for United States, metric, and Imperial (U.K.) measures. All Cooking Equivalent Measurements are approximate and most have been rounded up or down to the nearest whole number.

DRY/WEIGHT MEASURE				
		Ounces	Pounds	Metric
1/16 teaspoon	a dash	—	—	—
1/8 teaspoon or less	a pinch or 6 drops	—	—	.5 ml
1/4 teaspoon	15 drops	—	—	1 ml
1/2 teaspoon	30 drops	—	—	2 ml
1 teaspoon	1/3 tablespoon	1/6 ounce	—	5 ml
3 teaspoons	1 tablespoon	1/2 ounce	—	14 grams
1 tablespoon	3 teaspoons	1/2 ounce	—	14 grams
2 tablespoons	1/8 cup	1 ounce	—	28 grams
4 tablespoons	1/4 cup	2 ounces	—	56.7 grams
5 tablespoons plus 1 teaspoon	1/3 cup	2.6 ounces	—	75.6 grams
8 tablespoons	1/2 cup	4 ounces	1/4 pound	113 grams
10 tablespoons plus 2 teaspoons	2/3 cup	5.2 ounces		151 grams
12 tablespoons	3/4 cup	6 ounces	.375 pound	170 grams
16 tablespoons	1 cup	8 ounces	.500 or 1/2 pound	225 grams
32 tablespoons	2 cups	16 ounces	1 pound	454 grams
64 tablespoons	4 cups or 1 quart	32 ounces	2 pounds	907 grams

LIQUID OR VOLUME MEASUREMENTS				
Jigger or measure	1 1/2 or 1.5 fluid ounces		3 tablespoons	45 ml
1 cup	8 fluid ounces	1/2 pint	16 tablespoons	237 ml
2 cups	16 fluid ounces	1 pint	32 tablespoons	474 ml
4 cups	32 fluid ounces	1 quart	64 tablespoons	946.4
2 pints	32 fluid ounces	1 quart	4 cups	946
4 quarts	128 fluid ounces	1 gallon	16 cups	3.785 liters
8 quarts	256 fluid ounces or one peck	2 gallons	32 cups	7.57 liters
4 pecks	one bushel			
dash	less than 1/4 teaspoon			

CONVERSIONS FOR INGREDIENTS COMMONLY USED IN BAKING		
Ingredients	Ounces	Grams
1 cup all-purpose flour	5	142
1 cup granulated (white) sugar	7	198
1 cup firmly-packed brown sugar (light or dark)	7	198
1 cup powdered (confectioners') sugar	4	113
1 cup cocoa powder	3	85
Butter		
4 tablespoons = 1/2 stick = 1/4 cup	2	57
8 tablespoons = 1 stick =1/2 cup	4	113
16 tablespoons = 2 sticks = 1 cup	8	227

OVEN TEMPERATURES			
Fahrenheit (Degrees)	Celsius	Gas Mark (Imperial)	Description
225	105	3-Jan	very cool
250	120	2-Jan	
275	130	1	cool
300	150	2	
325	165	3	very moderate
350	180	4	moderate
375	190	5	
400	200	6	moderately hot
425	220	7	hot
450	230	8	
475	245	9	very hot

Please note that temperatures listed in these recipes were tested on a high-end Bosch oven. Temperatures or baking times may vary according to your oven's settings.

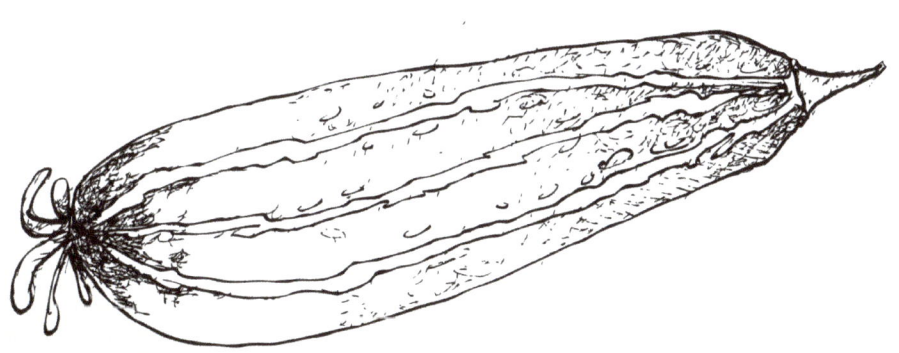

About the Author

CHRISTINA CAVALLARO EDICK

Christina was born and raised in Southern California. Growing vegetables in a backyard garden was part of her Italian-American heritage. She has a passion for cooking all things Italian and, because of an overabundant garden, zucchini. Christina loves finding new recipes, trying them out, and then tweaking them so that the recipe not only tastes better but easier to make.

When Christina is not in the kitchen she can be found traveling, with Italy heading the list. She shares her rich expertise giving food lectures, cooking classes, or demonstrations. Visiting wineries locally and abroad is yet another passion.

Check out her food and travel blog at:

https://christinasfoodandtravel.com

www.ingramcontent.com/pod-product-compliance
Lightning Source LLC
Chambersburg PA
CBHW061148070526
44584CB00034B/4458